I0627085

Un ERASED

ERASED

THE ATTEMPTED ANNIHILATION OF THE
JAMES WESLEY LAWRENCE LEGACY

BY JUDY EVE LAWRENCE-LAMB
DAUGHTER OF THE UNSUNG HERO

tph tucker
publishing house llc

Detroit Michigan

Copyright ©2025 Judy Eve Lawrence-Lamb

All rights reserved. No part of this book may be reproduced in any form, stored in a retrieval system, or transmitted in any form or by any means—electronic, mechanical, photocopy, recording, or otherwise—without the prior written permission of the publisher, except for brief quotations used in critical reviews or articles.

This book includes scripture from the New King James Version (NKJV), New International Version (NIV), English Standard Version (ESV), Amplified Bible (AMP), and King James Version (KJV) of the Bible.

Published by Tucker Publishing House, LLC

Paperback ISBN: 979-8-9917761-8-9

First Printing, United States

Endorsements and Words from
Those Who Knew James Lawrence

I share these words because I think that this is a beautiful representation of my dad's positivity.

"Mister Lawrence was a great man. He helped me get into public housing. I have known him all my life. He did a lot for all and everyone."

—Diann Knight-Worrell

Lifetime Friend and Neighbours

"God has a plan, and it seems like it's all coming together for you. Congratulations!"

—Eula Marshall

Family Friend

"You are more like your father than you could ever imagine, Judy. You have his strength and tenacity. He is so proud of you. Keep praying and pressing on the upward way...new heights you are gaining every day. Your bold sharing is helping many that you will never see, but keep the faith, and hang on in there. Just watch God open doors that

you thought you would never see. I'm proud of you. Your testimony has helped so many people. Pastor Shirley Caesar once sang a song titled Satan I'm gonna tear your kingdom down. Let nothing alter your heart. You have touched many lives and made them better because of your upbringing. You have shown kindnesses and prayers for others."

—Loretta Wood-Harrell
Former Secretary

Other Books by Judy Eve Lawrence-Lamb

Reaching Out: A collection of Inspirational Poetry

Sisters Without Color: A Celebration of Love

Delilah Goes to Church: She Is There to Give The Man of God a Haircut

Under One Roof: Multigenerational Living and Loving (Children's Book)

Patches (Children's Book)

Anthologies:

Words of Wisdom for the Heart and Soul Volume III (Cathy Staton) "Anchored Through Adversity "

Walking In God's Promises Volume IV (Cathy Staton) "God Promised: He Made A Declaration of Assurance"

Black Women Surviving Survivorship (Tara Tucker) "The Call That Became My Calling"

CONTENTS

Teaching American History with accuracy, transparency and NO erasures!

James Wesley Lawrence
UN-ERASED

#HIS-STORY #RESTORED
#ARCHIVED

James Lawrence shaking hands with
Dr. Martin Luther King in Peanut Park.

This book is dedicated to all the unsung heroes

FOREWORD

How do we measure the true impact of someone's life? I find myself returning to this question often, especially when I think of my own father and when I sit with families who have lost someone they love.

My father passed a little over a year ago, and I carry his memory with me every day. I still feel his presence in his living room when I glance at his recliner, he spent many of his last days resting in. I remember the smile in his eyes when he watched his grandchildren play soccer, and how he had a gift for making everyone he met feel seen and cared for.

Losing him changed me. Losing him irreparably broke me. Yet through the many tears and at times, debilitating hurt of his absence, I remain grateful and blessed that the most enduring things he left behind were not material at all, but the love he shared and the lessons he taught me.

True legacy lives in the love we give, in the memories shared by those who knew us, and in the values and stories we pass down.

I have seen that a person's essence continues on in the laughter at family reunions when their name is spoken, in the recipes they handed down for holiday meals, and in the way their children and grandchildren live out the principles they learned by example.

That understanding of legacy is what makes the story in this book so powerful. When I first learned of Judy, a devoted daughter who set out to preserve her late father's memory, I felt connected to her purpose. So, when I was invited to write this foreword, I felt truly honored to be a part of her mission to keep his legacy alive.

Her father was once a prominent figure in his community—a man who gave so much of himself to others. As the years passed, however, his name and contributions began to fade from public memory. But his daughter refused to let his story be forgotten.

Through her eyes and determined efforts, we see that his impact is still very much alive. She invites us into her journey of remembering, painting a vivid portrait of who her father was beyond the accolades: his character, his kindness, and the countless lives he quietly touched.

In these pages, Judy illuminates the true power of memory and identity in preserving a legacy. She shows us the way one life can ripple forward through others, even after that life has come to an end. As you read, you'll witness how the simple act of remembering and sharing a story can extend a person's presence into the future.

This book is a testament to how one person's values and spirit can live on in those who remain, growing and echoing through time and community.

Reading this story has affirmed my own belief that every life—no matter how publicly acclaimed or quietly lived—has inherent worth and a legacy that matters. I hope that as you journey through these chapters, you too will feel comforted and inspired.

And when you turn the last page, I invite you to take a moment to reflect on your own loved ones—the legacies they've left in you—and the ways you yourself are shaping a legacy with each day. May this book encourage you to cherish those memories and to carry forward the best of those who came before us.

Sabrina Winters,
Attorney at Law PLLC, Estate
Planning and Probate Attorney

AUDIO INTRODUCTION FROM THE AUTHOR

Audio Introduction

THE INTRODUCTION

Reflecting on the history lessons I've learned throughout my life; I realize that everything documented was not the documented truth. Many African Americans have been contributors to the history of this country only to have the acknowledgments go to undeserving individuals. They were individuals who had the knowledge, copyright, shared political interests and other tools to sabotage the blood, sweat and tears of the pioneers who toiled in the trenches. The accomplishments remain, while the ones who made them were erased.

Caucasian people who I will refer to as "white people" going forward, are often unfairly accused of underhandedly and single-handedly robbing these pioneers. Unbeknownst to many, a sad fact nevertheless, is that one of the tools used in the sabotage is another African American. You may ask yourself, "Why does this happen?" There are many reasons why—a few which include the crab mentality of seeing a crab crawl to the top and being dragged back down to join the others, envy due to personal insecurities or perceived self-inadequacies, the need to gain access to the pie in the sky even if it means standing on the back of the true pioneer, *or* just pure and simple ignorance.

I grew up in the era of Jim Crow and "tokens". It saddens me to realize that both spirits remain alive and well. They are strategically dressed up in kind acts and compliments, but they still exist in all of their glory. They have changed their attire from white hoods and sheets, overalls and plaid shirts to designer suits and pasted-on smiles.

I wrote this book because I have been fired up recently and the words that my dad, James Wesley Lawrence, one of those pioneers, planted in my spirit when I was a very young child, came flooding back to me. "Judy, if you don't stand for something, you'll fall for anything." Silence really is a form of consent.

I'd like to announce the death of Judy Eve Lawrence-Boddie-Chapman-Lamb (yes, all of them). She died of a broken and burdened spirit that she carried for decades. But the good news is that the wiser, more determined, bolder, more knowledgeable, radical and realistic Judy Eve Lawrence Lamb has resurrected in every way that matters. I tested the waters for thirty-eight years, and within that time, God gave me clarity. He pulled the covers, exposed the weights and the forces against me. He put my users and abusers under a flood light so that they could no longer be hidden behind compliments, fake hugs, fake smiles, fake handshakes, phony awards, accolades and concern. I was never truly celebrated; I was tolerated.

It was all meant for evil, but God used them for my good. God's timing, as always, is impeccable. He knew that being exploited was one of my weaknesses. I've seen so many of my people be exploited over the years, and God had to reveal the exploiters before He could carry out the plan He had for me—the plan that would take me to an expected end. When my exploiters were revealed, I confess that I felt pain because I truly believed that my love for them was reciprocated. Nothing was further from the truth.

I'm incredibly whole right now and, I have to admit, I could get used to this. It is through the grace of God that while my heart was broken by some friends and family, it does not leak. The same love I once had, remains. It's unconditional. I sincerely forgave them all, even if my forgiveness wasn't solicited. I had to do it for me because it wasn't their burden to carry; it was mine.

My dad's and my similarity went beyond our striking facial resemblance; I was also erased.

Stay tuned because the shackles are being removed, and I am about my Father's (father's) business. I have a charge to keep and a God to glorify! Ephesians 4:1-6.

In these pages, you'll find the history of my dad, the injustices of our people, some personal anecdotes, and encouragement to grab hold of your legacy, stand tall and proud in your true identity. Our history, in many respects, has been "white-washed" or erased.

CHAPTER ONE

THE LIFE OF JAMES WESLEY LAWRENCE BEGINS AND ENDS

God has ordained many and called them before they were even born. My dad was one of those called to change the world in a mighty way. As I sit and reflect on his life and legacy, I think of that little boy who had no idea of the huge impact he would have in this world. A little baby boy was born on February 14, 1917 (on a day that love is celebrated) to Charlie Wesley (27) and Leila Hurdle Lawrence (20)…a laborer and a housekeeper. His birth took place on Pitchkettle Road in Suffolk, Virginia, and his mother was assisted by midwife, Rosa Smith.

A little baby boy, who at seven years old found himself in the role of head of household and his mother's helpmate due to the absence of his father. He was a baggage boy at a grocery store.

A little baby boy who grew up to be a preteen and was often ridiculed for wearing the garments his mother sewed and his sister's shoes.

A little baby boy who grew up and was the salutatorian of his graduation class from Booker T. Washington High School.

A little baby boy who grew to be a man and became a Sergeant in the United States Air Force, took on a wife, later became a father to a baby girl and continued to be the provider and stabilizer for his mother and siblings.

A little boy who grew up to be the glue of his family—Who moved his little family from New York City to Suffolk and built a huge brick home in the neighborhood of Oakdale that included a beautiful hair salon with a waiting room for his young wife who had just completed beauty, culture school in New York City.

A little boy who grew up to be a pillar in his community and a target for envy, hate, harassment and persecution due to his commitment to the city of Suffolk. He was also the victim of KKK threats, endangering his wife and child, having to send them back to New York to ensure their safety.

A little boy who grew up to take on new challenges which included becoming the first housing manager, the first rehabilitation inspector, civil rights leader, and humanitarian for the city of Suffolk, all while maintaining his obligations to his own family by extending guidance and a helping hand.

A little boy who grew up and blessed so many people, died after securing his relationship with God, performing his last actions of kindness, setting a standard on which the city could aspire to reach and leave memories that time could not erase.

Young wife, Lucretia Lawrence who James Lawrence lovingly referred to as Wild Bill.

Little did the world know that that poor black kid—born of two uneducated parents on Pitchkettle Road could become a priceless citizen in the town of Suffolk? He didn't make it on his own; there were people who believed in him, and he spent his lifetime paying it forward. His childhood friend, Gene, labored at Planters to provide for his family, and Daddy saw great potential in him. As a licensed electrician, he educated his friend in electricity, and Gene became an A-1 electrician who worked side by side with my dad.

My father was gifted in seeing beneath the surface of an individual and bringing out the best in him or her. He did it effortlessly; it was who he was.

Little did he know that one day his little girl would grow up to write articles in the newspaper about him, run the household for him, support him in everything he was led to do and finally have a conversation with him about the necessity of rededicating his life to God as he aspired to lead God's people. Here's how the conversation went:

(Dad is preparing for bed and I enter his bedroom)

Me: Daddy, can I talk to you before you turn in?

Daddy: Yeah, is everything alright? Are you okay?

Me: I'm fine. I just want you to know how proud I am of you.

Daddy: Thank you, baby.

Me: Dad, I remember Aunt Bea and Ora telling me how you were an active member at Lakeview Baptist Church. They told me that you wrote poems for them like I do at Oak Grove. Is that true?

Dad: Yes, it is.

Me: What happened? Why did you stop?

Daddy: I got tired of going to church with a bunch of hypocrites.

Me: Daddy! You know that there are hypocrites in every church. Tell me—would you rather go to church with a bunch of hypocrites or go to hell with them all?

Daddy: Good gracious, Judy, that was intense!

Me: I guess so, but I've been thinking about what a big heart you have and how you are always thinking about the wellbeing of Suffolk. You can't lead them without the help of God. In order to effectively lead them, you have to follow Him.

Daddy: I can't argue with that. Goodnight, baby.

The next morning, he came to my room and asked me to iron his shirt. I told him that I wasn't aware that he had a campaign meeting. He told me that there was no meeting, that he was going to church. I felt like dancing!

A couple of friends of mine, Boss Man and Renee, had an automobile accident and needed a ride to church. Daddy was on fire! While the kids and I were getting dressed, he went to pick them up.

At church, I was in the choir looking out in the congregation at my favorite person in the whole world worshiping with me! It got even better! When Pastor Anthony Copeland opened the doors of the church, Daddy came to the altar. I can say that the following moments were like a dream come true. My daddy rededicated his life to God. He glowed! He came in and rolled up his sleeves. Daddy wasn't a warm pews kinda guy. He went to the city hall with members of the official board that Monday and led them straight into a blessing.

Three days later—that rainy Wednesday, he stopped by the house during his lunch hour. I offered to make him lunch, but he declined. He told me that he was going to Lowe's to pick up some building materials for an elderly couple in Lake Kennedy who could not afford to get their roof repaired and that he was going to find a roofer. He was doing what he often did. He was using his own resources. He wasn't a rich man, but he was definitely a benevolent man.

As he was leaving the house that day and got into the car wearing a cap, I remember saying to myself "I love that man." I will never forget that I was wearing a Michael Jackson tee shirt. After he left, I ran to get the Suffolk News Herald out of the paper box. As I stood in the living room reading the article that I had written about his candidacy for the City Council, the doorbell rang. It was one of the Mayfield boys who lived on Bunch Avenue telling me that I need to get to Portsmouth Boulevard because Daddy had just gotten hit.

I don't remember anything that happened before I arrived at the scene. I don't remember getting into my van, and I don't remember if I brought my children with me. I do remember seeing my classmate and friend, James Arrington telling me not to go to Daddy's car. He told me to go straight to Obici and give his information. I believe James was trying to protect me from the trauma of seeing him hurt.

Before getting back into the van, I was approached by the man who owned Paul's Auto, which was located on the corner of Portsmouth Boulevard. He asked if I was Judy. After telling him that I was, he continued by telling me that the impact of the crash knocked my dad's cap off. He put it back on, and after he did, my father said "Judy." That was his last word.

Recently, in the hotel room in Suffolk, my son, Allen, and I agreed that Daddy was on his way to Heaven, when he stopped by Oak Grove Baptist Church to reunite with his Father on Sunday and to be a blessing to the church on Monday, as well as to be a blessing to the poor elderly couple that Wednesday before stepping into eternity.

The question was asked in John 1:46, "Can anything good come from Nazareth?" Phillip replied, "Come and see for yourself." Today, I ask. "Can anything good come from Suffolk?" I bid you to come and see for yourself. James Wesley Lawrence was an imperfect man with a perfect love for God's people. He could have shaken the dust from his feet but until his demise, he chose not to. Matthew 10:14

Obviously, he wasn't Christ, but there is no question that he was Christlike. A standing-room only, out-of-the-door gathering of people at his homegoing service on March 23, 1986, was a testament of the lives he touched.

He lived out his calling by completing his assignment from God and was released from the troubles of this world to receive his reward.

CHAPTER TWO
HIS PAIN BECAME HIS PURPOSE

Those with high callings in their lives often experience great pain, and my dad was no exception. James Wesley Lawrence was a man who made sacrifices for what he believed in.

He never demanded respect, but because of the man that he was, he commanded respect. He never sought payback or recognition; those things he regarded as irrelevant. In his youth, his pulpit was under a house pulling wires for someone who couldn't afford an electrician, on a porch of a senior screening in the porch, sitting down with a student and challenging him to do his best in school or at his backyard fence encouraging a neighbor. When he became a senior himself, his pulpit was at the bank, withdrawing funds so that the same kinds of things would not go unattended.

If my father was alive and could read this book, it would never reach the bookshelves. He wasn't the kind of man who wanted to be celebrated. He would rather have been appreciated for who he was than for what he did. He was a man of integrity and that is what he was, effortlessly.

The plight of Black people was near and dear to his heart. He wasn't satisfied with being elevated while leaving others behind.

He and my mother, Lucretia, were a powerful team. They worked hand in hand together. In addition to being entrepreneurs—an electrician and a beautician—he held a supervisory position at Norfolk Naval Shipyard in Portsmouth, and she worked at Harrell's Meat House. It took her a while to realize it wasn't the place for spiked heels.

Daddy built our home with a beauty parlor and waiting room so that my mother could serve her clients in the comfort of our home. She was well sought out as a hairdresser and business was great. However, my mother refused to allow to have her clients' hair not done due to low finances. I believe that is why my parents were so blessed. Money was never their motivation.

When Daddy was working as a deputy for the sheriff's department, he came across a little boy who was shot by an uncle. I will call him Paul. He was hospitalized with no plan for when he was discharged. Daddy took it upon himself to take him in until he was securely placed in a proper home.

Then there was another little boy that I will refer to as Fred. He, too, was living in an inappropriate and dangerous environment. Daddy had decided to adopt him until he discovered that Fred was abusing me. He caught him twisting my arm and making me cry in the front yard. The one thing that he refused to tolerate was me being mistreated by anyone.

There was no such thing as Daddy being aware of someone's hardship and not doing all he possibly could to make things better. Often, it was a sacrifice, but it was often perceived as him being rich or without challenges of his own.

My friends loved coming to my house because they knew that the loving treatment I received would be the same they would receive also. Our home was a place of good times for some and refuge for others. It could be swinging on the backyard swings or having meals at our kitchen table.

Many adults were blessed by him as well. It would be from helping to find transportation to assisting in finding adequate and affordable housing, even if it meant opening the doors to our home and welcoming them in. Due to the fact that he was born and raised in poverty, he empathized rather than criticized.

He understood that a lack of education and often opportunity was like a millstone around the neck of some who couldn't seem to catch a break. He didn't assume that every impoverished situation was due to laziness and a lack of ambition. He knew the struggle and he knew it well. Was his kindness ever taken for granted? The answer is yes, but when he did the will of the Heavenly Father, his satisfaction was based on doing what was right; especially if children were involved.

Many times, when he went grocery shopping, I had to go with him. One basket was for us and the other was for a hungry family. Seldom did he shop for only us. To think about someone being hungry often took his appetite. I inherited that from him. When my children had friends over during mealtime and hadn't eaten, I would pretend not to be hungry so that they could sit and eat with my children.

It didn't matter what the need was; if Daddy was aware, it became his burden. It could be someone having a wood-burning stove and not having wood or someone not being able to pay an electric bill. He couldn't fathom having and not sharing.

He didn't enable people; he challenged them to do and be better. Sometimes that meant taking a young man under his wing and mentoring him. He was a wonderful encourager who recognized potential and was all in when it came time for his mentee to meet his or her potential. He always shared his humble beginnings to motivate that person who was ready to throw in the towel. He did not quote the Scripture, "To whom much is given, much is required" but he lived it. He lived it out loud! He firmly believed that if you give a man a fish, you feed him for the day; if you teach a man to fish, you feed him for a lifetime. He was the example because he realized that he could not lead where he did not go, and he could not teach what he did not know.

My Father's Benevolence Towards his Family

My parents were doting parents. They went above and beyond for me. They even went so far as to have my birthday party printed in the newspaper, giving the menu and the names of the chaperones and my guests. They had no limits to what they would do for their little girl. I remember my Christmases growing up. It was hard to believe they didn't have 10 children. When I think back to the Christmas mornings, I have to laugh because I went to their bedside to show them each gift that Santa had brought me. They were so good natured about it; they would oooh and ahhh at every single thing.

My dad was a great Christmas decorator, and my mom was a great cook. My home was the place to be during the holidays. My parents were a powerful team; they worked together. While Daddy ensured a well-built home with all of the bells and whistles, my mom would be decorating as she frequented Byrum's Hardware. She always dressed me impeccably from the Little Shop and of course my hair was always pretty. I remember being told that I had "good hair" like my father and grandmother. I wasn't sure what good hair was until I asked my mother for Shirley Temple curls. Because my hair was curly, she had to put a warm straightening comb to it. Daddy had a fit! I don't remember ever seeing him that angry with my mother when I was little.

Our Neighborhood

Oakdale wasn't fully developed when our home was built. There were no streetlights and we had dirt streets. My parents had a complete nightclub upstairs and they had socials to raise money for the makeover of our neighborhood. Even though my father didn't drink, I believe he had as much fun as anybody there!

My parents were very complimentary of one another. My dad was very handsome, and my mother was a knockout. They definitely gained a lot of attention when we were out together.

I had a beautiful and happy family, until I didn't. Suddenly, our happy times became less, and our sad times became more. It started with the KKK and our family being divided and our lives disrupted.

My mother was in the kitchen and about to make breakfast for my dad when she noticed a piece of paper at the door of her waiting room. She picked it up, and chills went through her as she read, "Niggers aren't wanted here." She called to my dad who came, read it and gave little response. He was a man of fewer words than actions. The action began when breakfast was skipped and a grassroot meeting took place on the Shipyard bus that carried Daddy to work every morning. He informed the passengers and neighbors of the note and everyone, including the bus driver, sprang into action.

That evening, 115 Carver Avenue became a battlefield. Neighbors were showing up with bats, handguns, and rifles. As they came through the front door, they made an immediate right and headed upstairs to join the others as they waited for the KKK. The newspaper was there according to my mother, and a picture was taken of her, Daddy, and me. My mom and I were taken away from our home and put on the Greyhound bus headed for New York City's Port of Authority. I slept through the trip and woke up at my cousin Louise's apartment on 116th Street. Going back and forth to and from New York wasn't foreign to me but I wanted my dad.

The End of a Perfect Union

The following years were a struggle for my parents' marriage. My mother began to hate the South and even though she lives with me in North Carolina, some of those feelings still remain. She's even triggered by wooded areas.

My mother's and my visits to New York became more and more frequent until my dad broke his leg as a result of playing football with the neighborhood boys. We were told that the breaking of the bone was audible.

This is when the decision was made for my mother to go to New York to work and to send money down while staying with her brother Eddie and his family. When things had finally settled down in Suffolk, my mother refused to return there. That was the beginning of my family's end.

I remember the day my dad showed up at the door in New York to take me home and they literally had a tug of war with me. I loved both of my parents, and it was breaking my heart; however, I was a daddy's girl through and through. After months of fighting, they decided to share custody of me. It was difficult for me; I never felt a part of any group of kids because before I was able to develop any strong relationships, I was always being pulled away. The only constant that I had in my life, with the exception of my cousins, was with my best friends, LaVerne Arnell Crocker and Synda Etta Knight. I remember my first job at the YWCA with the Harlem youth at 13. I didn't know my social security number, so I used the last four digits of Laverne's phone number, 6884.

The next big fight I remember between my parents was when I graduated from high school. My father wanted me to go to a local university in Virginia; my mother wanted me to go to State University of New York at New Paltz. I ended up at Bronx Community College working for First National City Bank at 111 Wall Street.

The night of the fight, I was so overwhelmed by it all, and at 18, I tried to take my life by taking a bottle of pills. When my mother came into the room; I was sitting in front of the vanity, and she wanted to argue with me. I told her what I had done, and she immediately called 911 and Uncle Eddie. We lived in close proximity to Harlem Hospital and his apartment, so they both showed up about the same time. Seeing my mother's and uncle's faces made me sorry that I had done it; I realized how selfish I had been.

When we made it to the hospital, my stomach was pumped and after being questioned extensively; I was allowed to go back home. My dad was never told about it because that would have been round two with my parents.

Things seemed to have gotten better once my boyfriend, Irving, was out of the Marines. Our focus was on our upcoming wedding which Mama took full control of. Irving and I enjoyed being together as he worked at Chase Manhattan at 55 Wall Street, down the street from where I worked. After the wedding, we moved to Queens on 144th Road. My mom had developed a certain attitude towards my father after their separation and complained about him coming to give me away, only bringing a watermelon.

Suffolk was the city of Daddy's birth, and the place where he worked tirelessly in order to provide for us. It was the place where he built the home of his bride's dream. Suffolk, in spite of his losses, was never erased from his heart. He died loving and serving it.

CHAPTER THREE

MOTHER, SISTERS, COUSINS AND A TEACHER TO THE RESCUE

N o truer words have ever been said than "It takes a village to raise a child." No matter what James Wesley Lawrence was engaged in, nothing came before his Judy.

There were two things people always said about us: *I was born with a silver spoon in my mouth* and *Daddy thought the sun rose and set in me.* Realizing that I needed constant nurturing from a female, he would call on Grandma, Aunt Bea, my aunt Ora, my cousins, Ann and T.C., Albert Jr. and Miss Amanda as well as my fourth-grade teacher, Mrs. Juanita Glover.

I had a special relationship with each of them. Grandma took me on trips in different states, made me pretty dresses, and taught me how to carry myself as a young lady, which included what

Lou Lawrence posing with James Lawrence's sister, Ora.

utensils to use when having dinner. She had a companion who was known in our Harlem neighborhood as the neighborhood's own Santa, Mr. Conway. He loved giving little children toys; his room was full of them, and I was privy to any toy my heart desired. He was well loved on 131st Street.

My aunt Bea never had children of her own, so she stepped in to nurture me. My aunt Ora loved to cook and make homemade ice cream. Later, she joined the church with me. My cousin Ann treated me like one of her daughters. She always thought that Daddy spoiled me, and she was right. He could never tell me "no," but when I was under her authority, I had to follow her rules. Albert Jr. was my cousin, but his wife, Miss Amanda, always treated me like she did her own children. Last, but certainly not least, was "my" Mrs. Glover, my fourth-grade teacher. My life began falling apart at the age of nine and she was there at the very beginning. She would take me home with her on Fridays, keep me for the weekend, and take me to East End Baptist Church on Sundays before my dad came to pick me up. I loved going to her house because she lived next door to my best friend, LaVerne.

My father never used corporal punishment with me. The worst thing in the world for me was knowing that I had, in some way, disappointed him. I don't ever remember him raising his voice at me, but he would become a wild man if he thought someone had physically or emotionally hurt me. My father was my safe place. He would applaud my victories and redirect my failures. If he needed the assistance from one of my nurturers, he did not hesitate to call. He never took advantage of them and was always benevolent to them. He was the go-to guy of the family. If he couldn't fix the problem, he would find someone who could. He was known for bringing tons of food through the doors of his loved ones. He would go to the bread store and load up on sweet treats. He would help with homework, encourage and motivate whenever needed, empty his wallet or just be present, no matter how tough the situation was.

He was cognizant of the fact that he couldn't be my everything, but he intentionally created a village to provide me with wholeness. He practiced what he preached.

I only have one memory of not feeling safe with my father and that is when I went into labor with my first child, Adrian. He was pacing back and forth, rushing me to come on, but I had no intention of leaving the stack of pancakes I was eating. I gobbled and screamed until finally I was in the car. He was driving like a madman and cursing the slow drivers as he headed to Obici Memorial Hospital. The medical staff was trying to figure out who was in the most need of attention—Daddy or me. Finally, I was rolled away, leaving a hysterical dad behind.

Irving, my husband, named the baby Adrian, and of course, I named him Wesley. Their temples are now side by side in Carver Memorial Cemetery while the two other "free" plots await my mother and me.

That was the plan until my son, Allen, purchased a place in the mausoleum for the two of us.

Even though I have had many tribulations throughout my life, I believe Daddy is at peace knowing that I am surrounded by people who truly love me.

Judy pictured with her first husband Irving, and
her firstborn son, Adrian.

CHAPTER FOUR

MY PARENTS' VOW TO ONE ANOTHER

Even though their marriage didn't survive, their promise to never divorce did. After all of the trauma was over, my parents became friends. When Mama would visit, I would walk in to find them sitting in recliners reading the newspaper like an old married couple. She would go into the kitchen and cook; he would sit down at the table to enjoy her cooking. When she turned fifty, he allowed us to throw a birthday party for her.

Several decades later, she still boasts about what an amazing and intelligent man my dad was. She occasionally has dreams, even now, of him and is still telling me how hungry she was after having me. She still speaks with annoyance of how she thought it was a turkey leg he was hiding behind his back when he came to the hospital, and it turned out to be flowers. She still talks about the way he put diapers on me that were falling off. She remembers him teaching me how to ride a bike in our neighbors', the Wrights, backyard. She has many beautiful memories, and it's difficult not to see moments of regret. They were a powerful couple with conflicting soul ties. Hers in New York. His in Suffolk.

Often, my mother would strike out at me because of my obvious dedication to my dad. Looking like him as much as I did didn't work in my favor either, in many situations. When things were good, she'd laughingly say, "You look just like that man!" When things weren't so good, those same words became accusatory, "You look just like that man!"

Not only did the vows of their commitment to never divorce remain, so did their unspoken commitment to giving me the best that life had to offer. My wellbeing was the one thing they always agreed on. Sometimes their perceptions differed as to what that was.

Being from a broken home doesn't always mean that one parent is missing; the home can be broken with both parents there and often, it is more painful for the child(ren).

Understanding this on the level that I did was my motivation to pursue my second Master's degree in family counseling. Unfortunately, I had to make a few hard decisions to withdraw after my first semester. My mother and husband needed more than what I was able to give, and they were, and still are, two of my top priorities. The good news is that at seventy-four years old, I have decided to make myself one of those priorities. I now read because I want to, not because I have to. If my body tells me to take a nap, I can; if it tells me that I need to move around, I move accordingly.

I learned a lot from the psychological lessons that were taught when I attended class; especially the fact that mixed messages from parents could lead the child to schizophrenia, known as the double bind theory. *Wow!* Was I ever blessed with the escape of that diagnosis!

My dad told me that he wanted me with him so that he could watch me grow up. On the other hand, my mom told me that there were no opportunities in Suffolk, and if you couldn't make it in New York, you couldn't make it anywhere.

However, God solved it on my behalf. Dad was always just being a dad. When I was with him, he'd help me with my homework, teach me life lessons; I would introduce him at speaking engagements, we would have breakfast together and just talk. He knew how much I loved cheese toast, and sometimes he'd make his own breakfast before going to work and I would often laugh and shake my head at him leaving cheese toast covered on the stove.

When I was with my mom, we had fun listening to music and her loving my dance moves, going to the movies, having fun at Coney Island or Palisades Amusement Park, or splashing in the waters of Jones Beach or Bear Mountain, going on trips and shopping like crazy downtown. My mom and I had fun together.

Between the two of them, my life had balance. It was just a shame that after having a beautiful brick home built for her, her making friends with coworkers, neighbors and clients and having a husband and child who adored her, she could not survive in an environment that was racist and threatening.

Lou and Judy on a cruise after the tragic death of
Judy's son, Adrian.

Some people judged her, but looking back, I began to realize some things about my mom. She was a very young woman who knew no more than what she had seen from the security of her apartment with her mother; she was married to a man twelve years her senior, who was forced to become a man at seven years old and had traveled the world by way of the United States Air Force. He wore many hats, and one was carrying the weight of his mother and siblings on his shoulders; I realized my mom was overwhelmed and possibly frightened by a reality that she wasn't prepared for.

Since reflecting on my mother and father, I've gained clarity. I remember when I was in my twenties. Like my mom, my mind was all over the place, but I had a dad to stabilize me—she didn't. My family suffered a deficit which became an asset to the city of Suffolk.

My parent's commitment to me never wavered, and they honored their vows by never divorcing, although they weren't "together" in the traditional sense.

CHAPTER FIVE

PRESIDENT OF SOUR (SAVE OUR UNDERGROUND RESOURCES)

I remember when people lived in houses with outside toilets and pumps in their backyards. Some of those houses existed right across the street from us. It was a part of Oakdale, but it was called Whitetown. The owner was a man by the name of Mr. White. We would see him walking from house to house collecting rent for the two-bedroom houses with no inside plumbing.

I was recently led to Google the neighborhood and found a description of Oakdale. It was described as a friendly and quiet neighborhood with friendly neighbors and well-maintained homes.

Riding through the neighborhood on one of our visits to Suffolk, everything seemed to be the same, with the exception of all of the properties being maintained. I couldn't help but visualize my dad calling a meeting in our home, serving drinks, food and encouraging his neighbors to bring our neighborhood back up to standards. Knowing him, he would remind the old residents of how it used to be and how they worked together to get lights, and the streets paved; he would challenge and encourage the newer residents to bring it back without them seeing it as judgment. He had a way of positively communicating with people without intimidation. Today, we have homeowners' associations (HOA) that have great benefits; however, there was never a need for it in Oakdale.

James Wesley Lawrence was a serious man, but he wasn't without humor. One evening he was speaking to a group of people who lived nearby in the middle- to upper-class houses and were staunchly opposed to the fight for inside plumbing in the impoverished communities. The audience became less vocal when he presented a scenario to them. He told them that the fly that rested upon a human feces in Saratoga (the impoverished neighborhood) was the same fly that traveled to Riverview which was their neighborhood and landed on a hamburger at a cookout. Needless to say, he got their attention.

When it came to saying what needed to be said, it was never a challenge for him; when he saw it, he said it with no apprehension. His commitment and support were not for sale. He was a man of strong convictions. He wasn't against an individual who stood in opposition to him; he believed that everyone was saved or lost by his or her own convictions and beliefs. He never judged, but he always made it clear any thoughts he had in any situation, expecting to receive the same respect. He willingly gave respect to a man's right to stand on what he believed—not excluding the Ku Klux Klan (KKK).

He realized it wasn't the actions that they performed because that wasn't within his control; it was how he responded to those actions, which was. If they felt their purpose called for them to mask up with hoods and sheets, and burn crosses, he had no control over those choices, but as the head of his household and a leader in his community, he knew that his purpose was to defend and protect the things that meant most to him—his family and his community.

Every time he went into his bathroom, decorated beautifully by his wife, he thought about his sisters on the other side of town having to go outside of their home, unprotected, to an unsanitary structure. And every time he went into his kitchen and turned on the faucet, he would think about his neighbors across the street who had to go outside to pump water.

These are the same people who paid rent or mortgage and state taxes. My dad couldn't wrap his mind around the obvious injustice of it all. Not only did his constituents and supporters listen to him; they heard him as clearly as he heard them. Save Our Underground Resources (S.O.U.R.) was just another platform on which he stood as the humanitarian and leader that he was.

CHAPTER SIX

PRESIDENT AND FOUNDER OF OAKDALE CIVIC LEAGUE

As the president and founder of his neighborhood civic league, and as a visionary, he saw the potential of Oakdale even though there were only a few houses surrounded by undeveloped and empty properties. When the roads were merely muddy potholes, he envisioned pavement on which cars could drive along the road and children could ride their bikes. When only the headlights lit the dark neighborhood, he saw streetlights that would illuminate the smothering darkness which would engulf the streets at night.

There was an empty field across the street where the children played baseball. Daddy had inspired them to clean it of trash and debris from passing cars and overall litterbugs with the vision of one day becoming a community park. However, sadly, he died before the vision came to fruition.

To show the importance of keeping a clean neighborhood and community, let me share a story with you. My daddy ingrained in us cleanliness and community. The day he was killed in the car accident, my son, Allen, before knowing what happened, got off the school bus, dropped his books on the steps of the house, but instead of entering, he ran over to the empty baseball field to pick up the trash. It was his daily routine, and he did it proudly and with excellence. Afterward, he came inside only to be met with the sad news of the passing of his grandfather.

Later, it became the home of Tabernacle Baptist Church which no longer holds services there. I can't help but see the vision of it becoming that home for the homeless that my father so desperately wanted for the city of Suffolk. I am definitely my father's child. I'm told that it's a gift, but honestly it feels like a curse when you can see something so clearly and others seem to be blinded and oblivious to it. I can identify with sharing dreams with such passion only to receive blank stares of disinterest. It sometimes makes you second-guess yourself and ask the question, "Am I overthinking?" Then there's a voice that softly speaks to me and tells me that timing is everything. It reminds me of *my* timing versus *God's* timing. God may be in the process of preparing hearts, minds, and spirits that will be a part of executing the vision—the vision won't die. Because people don't see it when you see it doesn't mean they won't get there. Preparations truly proceed blessings. We can't confuse God's timing with our perception of man's procrastination.

If God has anointed you to see beyond your circumstances, He may be preparing you for leadership because the fact is that you cannot lead where you do not go, and you cannot teach what you do not know. Sometimes God has to remove some spiritual cataracts, and sometimes the King Uzziah of our egos has to die in order for His Will to be done in our lives.

When my dad spoke with our neighbors about his visions of what our community could look like, he only wanted the visions to be seen and not himself. He recognized his limitations, but he also inspired them at their meetings to extend the boundaries of those limitations by reminding them that there was strength in numbers. In other words, one could put a thousand to flight, two could put ten thousand to flight, since it is the Lord your God who fights for you, just as He said He would (Joshua 23:10 KJV).

Watching the men of Oakdale work together helped me to recognize contentious relationships when I was confronted with them. They had no problem working together, even when there was a difference of opinion. I was raised to have the utmost respect for them because they earned it. With the Oakdale families, each child was each parent's responsibility.

The civic league meeting was a place to lay it all out on the table and to talk about it. After talking about it, there was mutual respect and, more often than not, a resolution. So, although there were many undeveloped areas, the community within thrived. We loved and supported one another. What my daddy did in Oakdale traveled to other areas as the Lord expanded his reach and territory.

CHAPTER SEVEN

VOTERS' REGISTRATION

D addy was an avid believer that each man, woman or child should always use their voices and to be present in the world in which they live.

I have so many memories of my dad and Mr. Moses Riddick when I reflect on the voters' registration movement. They were fully engaged in educating the citizens of the city of Suffolk on the strengths and weaknesses of the candidates and encouraging them to go out to the polls so that their voices were heard. There were few excuses as to why they couldn't because transportation was provided for them.

One thing that I clearly remember about my dad was that he had very high standards and he always challenged people who seemed to settle for mediocrity. The thing I most admired is that he not only challenged, he sought to equip them to meet that challenge.

Mr. Riddick and Daddy were very good friends; they fought many battles together. However, if there were ever any issues that they disagreed on, each of them took a firm stand. The battles they fought together were almost always a sure win; Daddy was referred to as the brainchild and Mr. Riddick, the bulldog. They were a formidable twosome. Those powerful men were definitely a force to be reckoned with.

I would see them working together and now decades later, I realize the passion that each of them had. Even in times of disagreements, it was obvious that the two men loved the city of Suffolk and were willing to talk it out—even when the volume went up as each of them made his point.

For some reason, I was never alarmed when this happened. Even as a little girl, I guess I realized that whatever was happening, it was happening between two men who had love and mutual respect for one another.

The conversation of voting began early in my life. I was not at the age when I disregarded the thoughts and opinions of my parents. Daddy always told me that if I didn't stand for something, I would fall for anything. Those words still resonate in my spirit when I am faced with adversity.

Looking back, however, after he was no longer here to guide and protect me, many times, I did not take a stand. If you were to ask me where there was an opportunity for improvement in my dad's parenthood, I would have to say that being overprotected by him crippled me because I became vulnerable to situations that could have ended my life. It was just that serious.

Once he was gone, I wasn't sure how to make a decision on who was best equipped to serve in whatever capacity politically because the intelligent, knowledgeable and educated voice in my life had been hushed in death. There were many missed opportunities to vote because I simply didn't know who I could trust. I didn't even trust my own voice.

I can't help but imagine having a conversation with my dad regarding the recent election of Donald J. Trump (Republican) against Kamala Harris (Democrat) in 2024. What would be his take on each side? Surely, he would have taken in consideration what was being offered and how it would inevitably affect the people of God. Would he focus on the economy, or would he consider the young child who may be forced to carry her father's child? Would the insurmountable cost of groceries be a major factor or maintaining peace within our nation? In making his decision, would he realize that the history of his people was in the making and how life-changing it would be to have a Black woman president of the United States? Would he remain a diehard Democrat, or would he balance the pros and cons of each?

There are times when not hearing my father's voice rings louder than a bullhorn. I trusted my dad and honored his opinion on every level. He is the only person that I can truthfully say that about.

Now that the election is over, I miss him even more because, in addition to being guided by him, he always had a positive reaction to whatever was happening. He taught me that man's extremities were God's opportunities. He taught me that things aren't always as they seem—that trials often distorted the triumphs.

I used my voice for election 2024, but it wasn't without apprehensions on both sides; however, I knew I had to perform my civic duty. Hearing about Project 2025 gave me chills. Abortion saddened me. The choice made by the government for making that decision rather than the woman carrying the baby angered me. I did not take this election lightly. It's important, regardless of what side you are on, to use your voice. My dad believed that, and so do I.

CHAPTER EIGHT

MY OPPORTUNITY TO BE HEARD
BEFORE THE CITY COUNCIL

Some of my healing began as I stood before the city council and realized that the present serving members had not had the opportunity to know my dad, with the exception of Vice Mayor, Leroy Bennett. They had no part of the erasure of his servitude, so my passion was just that, passion with no anger.

With butterflies in my stomach, but a resolve to keep going, fighting for my dad's legacy, I stood boldly and walked to the podium. I knew I had five minutes allotted to me, so even as I took the brave walk, with each wobbly step, I formulated the words. I didn't want to waste their time or mine, but *how could I put thirty-eight years into five minutes?*

I heard my voice speaking:

"Due to the emotional state I remain in after thirty-eight years, I choose to write the words from my heart. A memory came back to me. I came to Daddy's office one day located in Cypress Manor. While in his office, I saw his secretary and him lightheartedly joking. When he saw me standing at the counter, he referred to me as his protector. It was a joke at the time, but here, decades later, I have become just that. Not for him physically, but I must protect his legacy.

"My dad instilled in me the obligation to boldly take a stand for what I believed in and against the things I didn't. Daddy was the wind beneath many wings. His humility and true humanitarianism may have prevented the appreciation, celebration, and recognition that he earned and deserved. He was an unsung hero. Had there not been voices left behind, technically, he never existed.

"My father's lawyer advised me to have my mother transfer her rights as the administrator of my father's estate to me; after which, he became inaccessible. I trusted him because my father did. As a result of my trauma and lack of experience in such matters, it was brought to my attention that I was spending from a Railroad Retirement account that was supposed to end at the point of my father's death. I reached out to him several times with no response. My father trusted him to handle his business affairs, so I had no apprehensions of turning to him for counsel (as was suggested by the official who came to my home to inform me of this—he told me that the issue could easily be resolved).

"The lawyer's negligence to respond is questionable because, as Daddy's attorney, he had full knowledge of my father's insurance policies, investments and real estate. We were only given four "free" burial plots and a casket from the Suffolk Redevelopment and Housing Authority. In regards to the retirement fund, I was assigned a public defender who advised me to plead guilty to avoid having to leave my four children. I was found guilty of knowingly and willfully embezzling even though it was neither a knowing or willful act. I served a brief sentence and was labeled a felon. (I was working as an assistant teacher at the time and advised by my principal that I should resign to avoid being fired by the Suffolk Public Schools. It placed me in emotional and financial devastation. Not only was I robbed of my inheritance; I was robbed of the ability to provide for my family).

"Later, I was blessed to have someone who assisted me in making full restitution. My dad was on the clock when he was killed on Portsmouth Boulevard. When I was informed of my due inheritance, it was past the statute of limitations. Finances were not on my mind as I had just lost the most valuable and precious thing in my life—my dad.

"As an overwhelmed mother of four children who had been financially weakened, I thought that we were blessed by being "given" four burial plots. Perhaps it was a deterrent to prevent me from looking into his insurance policies. My only focus was providing my dad with a proper homegoing.

My dad was vigilant in seeking solutions. Article after article in the newspapers outlined specific plans addressing vacant buildings for the homeless, advocating for Suffolk which was vulnerable to the exploitation of other municipalities in regards to water supply, establishments for the purpose of giving our youth positive direction and many other visions.

"Cameras? No. He never sought to be seen. With exceptional intelligence and articulation, however, he commanded to be heard.

"The city of Suffolk has named streets and establishments in honor of certain citizens' contributions. However, James Wesley Lawrence—the city's first housing manager as well as the first rehabilitation inspector for the city, president and founder of his neighborhood's civic league, candidate for the city council, president of Save Our Underground Resources (S.O.U.R.), civil rights leader, one who endured threats from the Ku Klux Klan (KKK) in response to his taking a stand against racism, a humanitarian, a promoter and advocate for the wellbeing of the youth as well as the homeless, a visionary and an overall leader of the community—was somehow overlooked or more accurately, erased.

"No cameras captured him grocery shopping for hungry families, buying building supplies and hiring workers to repair the roof of a senior citizen couple in Lake Kennedy, buying school supplies for impoverished students, having the children in Cypress Manor to pick up litter on Davis Boulevard, motivating tenants who live in economically disadvantaged communities to plant flowers in front of their dwellings, being instrumental in bringing the Rev. Dr. Martin Luther King, Jr. to Peanut Park, selling a part of his property for $300 to a family moving to Suffolk with seven children, providing employment to those in a financial struggle, getting citizens to get out to vote while organizing transportation for them to do so, dealing with being a single parent when he lost the partnership of a New York wife who struggled with her husband's dedication to the city—all while making a difference in the midst of racism and token people of color.

"It disturbs me to have my grandchildren and great-grandchildren attending Suffolk Public Schools, oblivious to the contributions made by their great grandfather and great-great-grandfather in the city in which they live; especially considering the other generations of various other public figures who worked alongside my father. Those children are privileged to take pride in their families' history and legacy. Do the generations of James Wesley Lawrence deserve any less? Absolutely not!"

I went past my five minutes, and no one interrupted me. I turned and walked back to my seat, head held high, strong knees and a smile full of pride. I watched faces as I walked— faces of compassion. My grandchildren and great-grandchildren were in attendance at that meeting. They were young, but it was a moment—a moment that they won't soon forget.

The counsel conversed about what I said. Then the Vice Mayor spoke on my dad's behalf. It gave me much joy to have him acknowledge that Daddy's contributions should be considered when naming a street or a building going forward.

As I reflect on that night, I believe healing took place within my heart—healing that has enabled me to seek the acknowledgement and appreciation my father deserves.

Whether it's thirty-eight minutes, thirty-eight days, or thirty-eight years, one doesn't give up on what matters.

The Lawrence family pictured with Ex-Vice Mayor Charles Brown and CEO of Suffolk Redevelopment and Housing Authority, Patricia Tyrus.

Judy meeting with Suffolk City Council to honor her father with naming a street or building.

CHAPTER NINE

THE CAUSE AND EFFECT

Thirty-eight years later, people told me they thought I was rich. It never occurred to me that people assume my father had left me in great wealth. Even some city officials knowing of Daddy's assets thought that I had become rich after the death of my father. One of them was confused as to why I gave him the cold shoulder when I would see him. He thought that perhaps I was being careful not to be financially exploited by being guarded with my interactions. I thought that, like daddy's lawyer, he had turned his back on me—that when Daddy died, so did his affinity with the people he trusted.

I was being cautious, but not for the reasons he suspected. Little did he know, I was in a financial abyss. There were many nights that I had to sleep with my four children in order to keep warm because the oil had run out of the oil drum that supplied the heat to my home. My daddy's lawyer was supposed to help me secure what was rightfully mine, but instead he forsook me. He ghosted me. I could not get in touch with him. He never returned my calls, and I was left to figure things out on my own.

So yeah, I was careful, and to add insult to injury, I wasn't a tither, so I didn't qualify for help from my church. I literally had nothing to tithe. Ten percent of nothing is nothing. However, Mr. Rountree, the oil man on White Marsh Road and a deacon at my church, got wind of my struggles, showed up at my home, and filled our oil drum. I can't help but believe the generosity shown by Mr. Rountree was a karmic response to my dad's lifetime of kindness.

There were days when I only had Oodles of Noodles and a pack of Kool-Aid to feed my children. I would pretend not to be hungry because I wanted them to get enough. If they happened to have visitors over, I would divide what they had because seeing a hungry child wasn't something I could do.

I remember working under degrading circumstances where I was constantly sexually harassed and expected to pick dirty underwear off the floor or empty dirty bathwater for $100 a week. That money had to cover food, gas for my car, electricity, oil, water and the telephone. I can't, to this day, figure out how we survived, but through the grace and mercy of God, we did.

I remember one Christmas when my children didn't receive any gifts. We were, however, blessed with a Christmas basket filled with holiday fixings. I made a wonderful meal for my babies, and they even told me that it was the best Christmas they ever had.

My mother was in New York and had no idea what we were going through. I'm pretty sure she thought that Daddy had left me well off too.

She was shocked when she found out. She sent me a check to go Christmas shopping for the kids, and we had Christmas in February. From that point on, she began supplying us with what we needed. No matter what it was: clothes, shoes, oil, food, school supplies, light bill, telephone bill, and medications. She supplied our every need. She would keep my two oldest children for the summer in New York. While providing for them there, she continued providing for us in Suffolk. When my son, Adrian, became a father, she became a blessing to his children as well.

Now, I began to understand why everyone thought I was rich—it was beginning to make sense to me. I thought no one cared for us, they thought I was greedy, but in reality, I was in need. I had very little support from anywhere, and I never understood why.

I am a reasonably intelligent woman, but I didn't realize that grief could be so debilitating. It never occurred to me to ask about it. A man who lived a philanthropic life until moments before he died would leave a daughter that he cherished to fend for herself. Anyone who knew my dad would say that the thought of that was incomprehensible. We had a bond second to none. He covered me in every way possible.

I remember being stopped by the police one day after Daddy died. Everything on my car had expired. When the police informed me of that, I broke down in tears. My dad always took care of everything! Once again, God stepped in on my behalf and moved on the officer's heart with compassion. He instructed me to drive to a place called Blueberry Hill and park. He drove me home and told me to be sure to have everything done as soon as possible.

My angel was still watching over me. Monetarily, I was impoverished; but my dad left a wealth of love behind for me.

CHAPTER TEN

THE IRONY OF THE "FREE"
FOUR BURIAL PLOTS AND CASKET

When your primary source of income and provider, who is the heart and soul of your existence, is suddenly taken away from you, how do you respond? When I lost my dad, I fell into a cognitive coma. I blindly began to feel my way around the world. *I would never see the daddy I've loved and depended on all of my life again.* I couldn't breathe! That day as I sat in an office at the funeral home listening but not really hearing, I was numb.

The only thing I clearly remember was being told that the Suffolk Redevelopment and Housing Authority (SRHA) had paid for four burial plots in Carver Memorial Cemetery and a casket for Daddy. I had no clue as to why I was receiving three additional

plots; I was just grateful that I wouldn't have to worry about his. I felt ashamed that I wasn't able to give my dad the homegoing he deserved and was relieved as well as grateful that someone made the proper provisions for me.

Decades later, the question came to me, "Was the graveyard real estate in exchange for the inheritance that he labored for all of his life for the benefit of his posterity, and his insurance policy?" It blows my mind that I was so out of touch with reality that it didn't occur to me to ask. Looking back, I had to have appeared brain dead to the people I came into contact with. *Was I a dead woman walking?* Who loses a loved one and doesn't inquire about the insurance policy of the deceased?

Why were the "free" graves given to me? Could it be that someone didn't want me looking too closely into my daddy's affairs? Would it lead me to discover what was rightfully mine? What happened to his real estate, financial holdings, and insurance policies? Am I to believe that the highly intelligent mover and shaker, James Wesley Lawrence was uninsured? Could my grief have been so overwhelmingly devastating that it robbed me of my senses?

Things like this only happen on television; surely no one could possibly be smart enough to pull off such a heinous criminal act as seamlessly as this. *What did I miss? What would make a criminal think that he could pull it off?* That's the one question I do have the answer to. It was no secret to anyone in the city of Suffolk the kind of relationship Daddy and I had. So, it is reasonable to assume that I would be so devastated that I wouldn't question his lawyer. I was the one true constant in his life along with my little sister, Alisa (Lisa), and he was mine. His pain was my pain. His happiness was my happiness. With the exception of God, no one loved either of us more.

So, to say that I was robbed of my inheritance is an understatement. My sister lost the home that Daddy built for her, but at least we could trace the loss and account it to something. I know without a shadow of a doubt that my father's plan was to leave Lisa and her baby, Travis, a home in Chuckatuck, and me the family home that he and my mother had built together in Oakdale.

I would like to thank SRHA for the free real estate in Carver Memorial Cemetery; my dad's and my firstborn's bodies lie at rest there. My mother and I appreciate relieving the burden from my children, and we intend to be there as our final resting place, but in the meantime, I'm on a mission to take back everything that the enemy stole from me as I live and breathe. If God calls me home before that mission is accomplished, rest assured, the plan of action isn't mine alone.

We will not settle for the graves being his only real estate and the casket being his only home. What was done in darkness is about to come to the light. Covers are about to be pulled, and may Heaven help the exit of the skeletons in the closet.

I have decided that it is time to take back everything that the devil stole from me. Free real estate in a graveyard is hardly comparable to my dad's assets.

The Lawrence family pictured in front of the Oakdale home.

CHAPTER ELEVEN

THE PAINTED DOLL

Daddy showed his intolerance when he painted a little white doll of mine. I was raised to respect all people, regardless of race, creed or color. I didn't know there was a different race of people than myself. I just thought people had different complexions because it was normal and just the way it was; we had various complexions within our family. My mother had a very fair complexion, and my father had a very deep complexion. My aunts, uncles, cousins, friends—all varied, and I was oblivious to anything other than their kindness towards me.

I remember, one day, my mother and I were heading to New York. We were at the old Suffolk Railroad Station. My mother went ahead of us and boarded the train to wait for me while Daddy and I had one of our long goodbyes. She was sitting close behind the conductor in the front seat. When my dad finally took me to the train and I sat beside my mom, we were asked to go to the rear. I remember staring at the empty seat during the whole trip, not understanding why we had to move.

One day, I was in uptown Suffolk with my aunt Bea. As we turned the corner of the large bank that stood there, a little white boy looked at me and stuck out his tongue. I didn't equate that to racism because that was a foreign concept; I just saw him as a mean and rude little boy.

Also in Suffolk, I remember my mother and me being at High's Ice Cream store. Mama asking for chocolate ice cream cones for us and having to repeat it over and over. Suddenly, the white saleslady said, "Oh you mean choklate!" She laughed with her coworker at my mother's northern accent.

There were various times when racist things took place that I was oblivious to until the KKK, the poor whites and a few others that hated Blacks began to get bolder and more obvious. One night, the KKK threatened us with a note saying they were going to kill our family. They also placed a cross in my yard. My mother showed it to my dad. I didn't see my dad make any expression but later found out he shared it with the neighbors. They came to our home with guns and weapons. They all positioned themselves, prepared to protect us and our home. I was seven years old when the rose-colored glasses fell off and I was awakened to the racism all around me. Suddenly, all the previous incidents made sense. We were discriminated against on the train, and in the ice cream parlor. Even the little mean boy was showing racism toward me. I saw the community come together and the love that they showed toward us.

Lou Lawrence celebrating 50th birthday with friends in dance hall of Oakdale home.

One day Daddy came home with a bucket of varnish. I wasn't curious about it because he was always working on some sort of project to beautify our home. He had bought me a beautiful walking doll. As I moved her hands back and forth, she walked. She was very tall and almost lifelike. She was like a very close friend to me, and as an only child, I appreciated having her with me during the day. I loved that doll! You can imagine how horrified I was when I discovered that the varnish was to paint my doll. Daddy had had enough! Perhaps, I was too traumatized to remember after that what happened, but I'm sure he found a way to help me recover.

He was very protective of me and my wellbeing; so much so that he turned our garage into a very elegant dancehall where my friends and I could safely enjoy dancing, listening to our music and having fun. I remember the master control panel behind the beautiful bar he had built so that we could hear music in each room of the house. The dances at Booker T and at the Union Hall couldn't compare to the dances at Judy Lawrence's house. It was the place to be! I laugh as I write this because the boys knew to behave themselves.

It didn't matter if he had to paint a doll, build a dancehall, buy a car, be my chauffeur or lay somebody out who dared to strike out at his baby, when it came to me, James Lawrence could be quite interesting. Just as he taught me to be respectful to all people, he expected no less when it came to me receiving the same level of respect.

CHAPTER TWELVE

THE DIVERSITY OF JAMES WESLEY LAWRENCE

My dad was a man of many talents. Whatever the challenge, he pursued it with bold and focused vigor! The old cliche, "Jack of all trades and the master of none" definitely didn't apply to Daddy. He mastered everything he attempted because he knew where his strength was.

First, at seven years old, he became head of his household to assist his mother. He made provisions for his family with his small salary from bagging groceries. They were a poor family who had very little of anything but enough of everything, thanks to him and my grandmother. He tutored them to ensure that their intelligence wouldn't be hindered by their poverty.

Even though his attire wasn't up to par, and he was often teased when he attended school, he graduated from Booker T. Washington High School as his class's salutatorian.

He was a brilliant student, and history was his favorite subject. When he grew up, he joined the United States Air Force where he was a sergeant. He was at Pearl Harbor on the day it was bombed. One day, he was called a nigger. Things escalated and he was honorably discharged. I don't know the details, but I'm sure Daddy's response wasn't a peaceful one.

Then he went to school and became a master electrician, starting out at the New York Subways and ending up as a shop steward at Norfolk Naval Shipyard in Portsmouth. He was also a very successful entrepreneur of electrical work. He was a member of Suffolk's Planning Commission and would actively challenge the minds and visions of its members. Daddy was the founder and president of the Oakdale Civic League, and an activist for voter registration. He was a prominent leader and an active member of the NAACP, as well as spokesman.

As mentioned in a previous chapter, he was the first housing manager for the city as well as its first rehabilitation inspector. When he closed his eyes and stepped into eternity from a highway in the city he loved, he was a formidable candidate for Suffolk City Council and was in the process of helping his fellowman until the minute he died. At sixty-nine years old, he accomplished more than 100 years of service.

Daddy was an imperfect being on a perfect mission. He did not allow his age or responsibilities to hinder him from meeting challenges head on. It could never be said that he was a "jack of all trades and a master of none." He mastered every project he attempted to undertake.

CHAPTER THIRTEEN

WHEN MY HEART BROKE INTO
A MILLION PIECES

Daddy finally found love after five years of separation from my mom; she was a much younger woman. I believe her youth energized him, and he wanted to give her a world she never knew. Before she came into our lives, my dad was alone, but he didn't seem to be lonely. He would do what he usually did before he and my mother separated. He would go to work, come home, have dinner and watch the news until bedtime.

When Marion came into our lives, I loved her immediately. We spent most of our time together cooking, joking around, and playing records. She was fun and she brought a different energy to our home. She would keep my secrets from Daddy; I could tell her anything. Then to everyone's surprise, she became pregnant, and after almost 18 years of being an only child I was over-the-top happy at the anticipation of being a big sister. I loved seeing her stomach grow bigger and bigger with my sibling. Those were the days when you didn't know whether it was a boy or a girl until the baby was born.

Finally, the day came when she would become a mother and I, a big sister! Daddy, Marion's mother, Idabell, and I took her to the hospital. I was told to sit in the waiting room until they got back, but that wasn't going to happen. As soon as they were out of sight, I ran to the elevator and went to the third floor. I was going to be the first to see my baby sister or brother! I made it to the room before they did. They both laughed at my determination.

From the moment I laid eyes on her, I was in love. Marion didn't get much opportunity to bond with her little girl because I completely took over. I remember one night when we couldn't find her pacifier and she was crying a lot. Marion was angry with me and whatever it was she said to me, it hurt my feelings. I was upset and went back into my room to go to bed.

The next morning, I went to tell her that I was sorry and saw that she had been crying because she knew that blaming me for the lost pacifier had hurt me. There was mascara all over her pillowcase. From that day on, we never had a disagreement about Lisa. She supported our relationship so much that she allowed me to name her. When I was 13 and working at the YMCA in New York as a jr. counselor, one of the kids I worked with was named Alisa. I loved that little girl so much and always said if I had a little girl, her name would be Alisa. I wanted her middle name to be Romaine; not that I liked the name, but I was being mischievous. My dad's baby sister was pregnant at the same time Marion was, and she said that if she had a little girl, she would name her Romaine. We were always in competition for one reason or another so I beat her to the punch. The funny thing about it was she ended up having a boy and naming him Warren. So much for beating her to the punch. Later, I realized that I had named my little sister after a head of lettuce. Poor Lisa.

When I decided to move back to New York, I really missed my little sister. I would send her cute little outfits and talk with her on the phone, but that wasn't enough. I talked my husband into leaving New York and moving to Virginia. As far as our marriage was concerned, that was a huge mistake. We didn't realize at the time that I was in the process of having a miscarriage. I was heartbroken because that was our second miscarriage. I went to Lakeview Clinic and was advised not to get pregnant again right away, but I wanted a baby so bad.

We started out staying with my dad, but he had been building another house on our property, right behind the main house. When it was completed, he handed Irving and me the keys. It was a very nice house. Soon after moving there, I discovered that I was pregnant again. This time, I was hopeful because I had gotten past my first trimester. I began to get excited as my tummy got rounder.

At that time, neither Marion or I drove, and we would enjoy walking from Oakdale to Suffolk Health Department, which is across the street from where North Main Street Walmart is now. It didn't seem far to us because we laughed and talked the whole way.

We left Lisa with her grandma, IdaBell. The lady that checked me in was Mrs. Annette Ruffin. Years later, Mrs. Ruffin and I became 'church family.' I was actually her assistant as she served as church clerk at Oak Grove Baptist Church. She always encouraged me. She made me laugh when she told me that she used to have a crush on Daddy when she was younger. I still miss her to this day. I hate that she never got to write her book; she was a very wise lady. I digress.

Marion was very protective of me. I started out ninety-nine pounds when I first got pregnant and by my due date, I was weighing 181. My stomach was huge, and my belly button stood out. When Marion would see someone staring at it, she would lay them out. "What the hell are you looking at!" That was my Marion.

When I went into labor with Adrian, she was right there, trying to pull me out of the house away from a pile of pancakes. I had heard that they wouldn't be feeding me until after the baby was born, and I wasn't taking any chances. My husband was working at a place in Norfolk on Granby Street called Cal's Closet, but they couldn't locate him so Daddy drove me to Obici Memorial Hospital fussing at the slow drivers all the way. He and Marion immediately fell in love with my little nine-pounder. No wonder I had gained so much weight.

As Lisa began growing up, and with Daddy still legally married to my mother, he didn't want Lisa not to have a home built for her. So, he bought some property in Chuckatuck and built a home for her and Marion—somewhere to call their own. That was the beginning of 142 Pembroke Lane. It was a pretty, little brick home, and Marion was very proud of it. For years, I enjoyed going there and listening to music in their downstairs sitting room or going to Lisa's room to play with her.

When she got older and tried to play hooky from school, I would receive a call. Immediately, I would hop into the car and take off to Chuckatuck. Finally, she gave up and began going to school every day. They never thought to give me a key, but I would bang on the windows until she let me in.

Once when I wanted to spread my wings, under section 8, I moved to a four-bedroom apartment in Heritage Acres. My dad helped me to get settled in and would make sure that I had everything I needed for the children and me. He would bring bags and bags of goodies to us.

One night, Daddy stayed over and slept on my couch. Of course, he was welcome, but I couldn't help wondering if Marion knew where he was. He never told me, and I never asked.

One day, as I was passing Oakdale, I decided to stop and look in at the house. When I entered the kitchen, my heart felt as if it had stopped beating. On the floor, in front of the sink was a blanket, and beside it was an alarm clock! It didn't take me long to realize that my daddy had been sleeping there. He and Marion had separated, and she had gone on with her life. Because that home was built for Lisa, he felt he no longer should insinuate himself there. I was living in public housing, so he couldn't live with me. Our home was under reconstruction with no furniture, so the kitchen floor became his place to rest.

This was a very difficult chapter for me to write because I am literally feeling a weight in my chest that causes my breathing to become labored. This is why I can't stand idly by and once again see the fruit of my father's labor erased. I will unapologetically stand in defense of Dad's honor and his kind heart. He deserves no less.

James Lawrence's two daughters, Judy and Alisa.

CHAPTER FOURTEEN

DADDY, THE OVERLY PROTECTOR AND ENABLER

D addy was a force to be reckoned with. He was known as strong, courageous, intelligent, and radical, but when it came to me, he was a proverbial teddy bear. When Alisa came along, he realized that he had not been properly preparing me for the real world, and he was better at it with her. But with me, the monster had been created and nurtured. If we would have to spotlight one of his downfalls, this could definitely be one of them. My father would be the first to own up to missed areas of opportunity for improvement when it comes to himself. He never thought more highly of himself than he should. His mission was to protect me from every bump in the road, not realizing that the bumps would prepare me for the hard times that were ahead of me. He never considered the day he would be taken from me and how vulnerable I would be.

Daddy had so much life in him that I guess he didn't really think about the alternative. When I think about it, it wasn't a bad perspective. He lived life in the moment with his eyes always open to the future. I wonder if Daddy was aware that he was performing within the boundaries of God's Plan, allowing me to endure what I needed for God to bring me to my preordained destiny? Who knows?

There was a time when I was staying with my cousin, Ann Taylor. My cousin, who I endearingly referred to as my sister, Brenda and I were going to a dance at the Union Hall. We were so excited about going! My mother had sent me two really cute minidresses from New York, one red striped and one blue striped. Brenda and I got dressed in them! We looked absolutely adorable. I remember standing in front of the mirror and my little cousin, who I also referred to as my sister, Vanessa, told me that I was pretty. I will never forget that compliment because I believe she really meant it.

It was a rainy night but suddenly began to pour with thunder and lightning. Cousin Ann came to the room and told us that we weren't going. *Oh no!* I sneaked and called my dad, crying about how disappointed I was. Of course, he came to pick me up, carried me to the dance, walked me in, went back to his car to wait, took me back to Ann's afterwards and kissed me goodnight. I can assure you that Ann wasn't happy with Daddy or me.

There was one time when I bounced a $100 check and neglected to pay it. I don't remember how I ended up in court, but Daddy had Mr. Robert Gillette as my attorney. The judge slapped me on the wrist and warned me that going forward, I was to handle my finances more responsibly. The irony of that was I had just been hired at the Bank of America as a teller.

When I became a young woman and began experiencing the normal changes associated with puberty and didn't know what I was supposed to do, he called my aunt Bea for instructions, went to the drugstore for the supplies, came back home and together, we did what needed to be done.

About thirty-one, I lived on my own. I lived in an apartment just off the road where my dad was killed. I was raped by the maintenance man. I called my dad, and he came packing a gun! Thank God, the maintenance man was nowhere to be found. But I didn't let this go.

Again, I found myself in court with my dad. When I saw my rapist sitting in court with his wife and seven children sitting behind him, I pleaded with Daddy because of the compassion that filled my heart looking at his babies. I couldn't imagine them growing up without their father. At that moment, it wasn't about me. I settled for aggravated sexual assault. I hated what he did to me, but seeing the faces of those children got to me. I'm sure it was my rapist's strategy but nevertheless, seven children would have been left fatherless with only a single mother left with the struggle of raising her children alone. My heart wouldn't allow it. He was placed on probation and I never heard from him again. I did find out later that he was fired from the apartment complex. It was then that Daddy pleaded with me to move back home, and I did. That is where I remained until he died.

When my dad passed away, it wasn't easy living there and dealing with the memories, so I decided to move to another home he owned at 224 Cedar Street. Friends of mine were renting there at the time, and I hated asking them to find another place, but 115 Carver Avenue was no longer my home of joy; it had become a house of pain.

No more getting food ready to serve dinner as soon as Daddy walked through the door from work. No more Daddy walking through the house shutting off lights while fussing about waste. No more cheese toast being left in the oven for the kids and me. No more making me coffee. No more hearing him telling me what a good daughter I was and how proud he was of me while sitting with him in the downstairs living room. No more seeing him watch the news or a football game. No more seeing him engrossed in reading the newspaper. No more seeing him having an encouraging conversation with someone while standing in the yard or sitting on the front porch. No more watching my youngest children, Allen and Nichole, teasing him by tickling him and saying, "He's a pretty little boy" as he fans them away, smiling and trying to get away from them. As joyful as our home was, when he died, it was a hundred times more painful.

I couldn't cope! My protector, my guidance, my everything, with the exception of God, was gone, and he was never coming back. I ended up leaving Cedar Street which had a mortgage and allowing my estranged husband to live there while I pushed past the pain and returned to our Oakdale home that had been fully paid for for decades. I thought that the Cedar Street's mortgage was being paid until I was faced with a foreclosure. It was as if no good deed went unpunished. I felt that my whole world was crashing around me as I tried to give my children at least a portion of the security my father always gave me. I was a full-grown woman, responsible for four children, little-to-no income and living in a world that I hadn't been prepared for.

YouTube channel

www.judywrites.com

My dad's office.

Cypress Manor Apartments
in Suffolk, VA

Candidate Lawrence opposes 1-school plan

James W. Lawrence

By DAVID HARRISON
NEWS-HERALD REPORTER

City Council candidate James W. Lawrence said Friday he would not support a consolidated high school in any form, and called for the expansion of existing facilities at Forest Glen, John F. Kennedy and John Yeates high schools.

Lawrence, running in the Cypress borough, became the second council candidate to publicly oppose the plan for consolidation, which had its concept – but not funding – approved by current council members.

Wednesday, Suffolk borough candidate John Faircloth said he would not support the one-school plan, and said new elementary schools are a higher priority than a new high school.

Lawrence said, "If you take away all of Kennedy's special classes, and use it as the high school it was designed for, it could accommodate all the students who need to be moved out of Suffolk High School."

He said even though City Council has approved the one-school concept, "I would not vote for funding of one or two new high schools."

Lawrence is seeking the seat on council currently held by Vice Mayor Ronald O. Hart. The vice mayor

voted against the one-school plan, but the measure was approved by a 4-3 vote in December.

"This warehouse they're talking about would be obsolete before construction is even finished," Lawrence said, "and there's no way anyone in the city believes this plan will make it easier for kids to get to school."

Lawrence also said a large "warehouse" will make it more lucrative for major drug dealers to come to the school, having more students as prospective buyers.

"It would be an invitation to major dealers to come into the area."

Lawrence said teacher salaries must be raised in order for Suffolk to compete with school systems in other localities.

Lawrence, 68, is a housing manager who is making his first bid for council.

He has also stressed the importance of preserving many of the city's substandard housing facilities for possible use as temporary shelters for the homeless.

Another issue he said he will stress is the lack of activities for young people in Suffolk. Lawrence said the city should establish a center where youth can enjoy "wholesome recreation as an alternative to hanging around fast-food outlets."

Your view: Special classes

"It would appear to me that a candidate for City Council (James W. Lawrence) should know a little more about our schools." See Page 4.

-Election-

Continued from page 1

Goodman said the city needs to upgrade its recreation facilities, particularly tennis courts and playground equipment.

A third Cypress challenger, Wong-Ya Guillermo Jones, announced his candidacy yesterday. Jones is paralegal specialist working in Portsmouth, as well as a student. He was unavailable for comment this morning to discuss his stance on city issues.

Vice Mayor Hart, a teacher in the Norfolk School System, has stressed the need to increase the city's recreational facilities, and was the only councilman or council candidate to attend a recent Parks and Recreation public hearing.

"There are so few things for our young people to do," Hart said after the hearing, "and we have to come up with a way to provide them with well-organized recreational areas." Hart, 43, has also said sewage facilities and improved housing are major keys to progress in the Cypress area.

All three Cypress borough candidates oppose the single high-school concept.

In the Chuckatuck borough, incumbent Edgar Ray Savage is opposed by Bennett's Creek pharmacist Steven "Chris" Jones, 27.

Jones has questioned a number of council's decisions concerning future development and growth, stressing, "We're not Virginia Beach, and and we have to make sure growth occurs in a manner that's conducive to what this city is all about."

Savage, 40, is the last remaining farmer on council and will be shooting for his third term. Last month, Savage led a council charge to remove City Manager John L. Rowe Jr., and he has been the most outspoken critic of city policies involving growth, personnel, and spending practices. Savage and Hart were the only council members who opposed a 100 percent salary raise for councilmen included as a late addition to the last city budget.

Savage said advances in education are his primary goal as a councilman, and he voted in favor of the one-school concept. Jones said he will not commit himself on the issue until after the election, but he has said he doubts a single school would work considering Suffolk's current growth trend and its immense area.

Dentist William H. Higinbotham Jr., 51, is seeking a second council term as a Suffolk borough representative, and he will be challenged by Suffolk Olde Towne Civic League founder John B. Faircloth.

Faircloth, 44, has stressed a need for the city to work with the Suffolk Redevelopment and Housing Authority to help revitalize the downtown business district, as well as individual residences.

Faircloth also said city facilities must be improved, and called for pay increases for teachers.

Also challenging for the Suffolk seat is former Suffolk assistant school superintendent Benjamin L. Davis, who said housing, unemployment and economic development are all problem areas which the city needs to address and correct.

Davis, 68, said, "There's no way to overstate the importance of bringing in new business and industries, to bring in revenues and to create jobs."

Higinbotham said water and sewer extensions have been major points of progress for the city during the past two years, and he said housing and neighborhood preservation are major goals for the next term.

Higinbotham favors the school board proposal for one school, while Faircloth said he would vote against the concept and the funding for the project. Davis lobbied against the proposal when it came before council, but said he would be reluctant to reverse the vote since council already approved the concept.

79

Last minute filer creates four-way race in Cypress

Wong-ya G. Jones

By DAVID HARRISON
NEWS-HERALD REPORTER

An eleventh candidate slipped into the council race at the eleventh hour Tuesday, making the Cypress borough the most hotly contested in this year's campaign.

Wong-ya G. Jones, 31, a paralegal specialist at a Portsmouth law firm, filed just before the Tuesday afternoon deadline. He said he hopes to develop better relations between city departments and residents.

He also said the city should increase the number of facilities available to teenagers and children to give them "an alternative to hanging out on the streets."

Jones is running in a borough race which includes incumbent Vice Mayor Ronald O. Hart, local housing manager James Lawrence and air traffic controller William Goodman.

"We need to have a more tightknit community," noted Jones, who said the police department and city can work better with the people to increase a "sense of belonging in the community."

Jones said unemployment is one of the city's biggest problems, and he said Suffolk needs to make a greater push to bring in outside businesses.

"We need to knock on doors and take the time to approach all of the developers in the other parts of Tidewater, and sell them on what we have."

The Reed Court resident said creating jobs is essential if the city is going to keep its young people in Suffolk when they seek employment.

Jones lives just across the street from Goodman, and he praised his neighbor for his help and inspiration as he considered running for council.

See JONES, page 2

Jones

Continued from page 1

He said Goodman, as well as Hart and Lawrence, is "very capable" of serving on council, and said Hart should consider a larger goal, such as working in the General Assembly.

For himself, Jones aspires to be the first black vice president of the country, and gives himself about 20 years to try to fulfill that task.

"I know it's my calling to serve the public," Jones said. "I have seen where I'm going—and the place to start is at home."

Jones addressed some education issues, saying he does not like to see children separated in school based on abilities, stressing they need to work together to help each other.

He said the consolidated school issue is "probably a dead issue" because the school has already been approved by council. He said he is opposed to putting the high school into an educational park with Paul D. Camp Community College, which he termed "a private corporation looking for extra funds."

81

James W. Lawrence

Housing manager Lawrence dies in wreck

Housing manager James W. Lawrence died yesterday from injuries he received in a traffic accident on Portsmouth Boulevard during a heavy rainstorm.

Lawrence was stopped in the middle of the eastbound lanes of Portsmouth Boulevard waiting to turn left from Suburban Drive when his 1985 Chevrolet was hit in the driver's door by a car driven by Michael E. Berman, 32, of Virginia Beach, according to police reports.

Police said that Berman's Mazda was going 40 mph when it struck Lawrence's car at about 3 p.m.

Lawrence was taken to Louise Obici Memorial Hospital, where he was pronounced dead of internal injuries at 4:30 p.m., according to police reports.

Berman was treated and released in the emergency room at Obici.

According to police reports, charges in the accident, which is still under investigation, are pending.

Lawrence, 69, lived in the 100 block of Carver Avenue.

Funeral arrangements are pending with Crocker Funeral Home.

Life of 'hard work, decency'

STAFF REPORT

Many city residents are still in shock this afternoon after housing manager and City Council candidate James W. Lawrence was killed in a two-car accident yesterday.

Lawrence, 68, was housing manager for the Suffolk Redevelopment and Housing Authority, and had served on the city's Planning Commission and Board of Zoning Appeals.

According to police reports, his car was struck in the driver's side as he attempted to make a left turn onto Portsmouth Boulevard from Suburban Drive.

Lawrence was one of the best-known and best-liked figures in Suffolk, known for his work to improve housing conditions.

"The city has lost a great asset, a great citizen," said V. Janette Rountree, director of Suffolk Redevelopment and Housing Authority. "If there ever was a Mr. Suffolk, Mr. Lawrence was certainly in the running. We know his efforts to get housing for people of Suffolk of all incomes. We know his work to get underground utilities.

"But Mr. Lawrence, as an individual, touched so many lives, not as a diplomat, not as a civic leader, but as an individual. His ability to work with people and to relate to people was unsurpassed in this city.

"He will be sadly missed," noted Mayor Andrew B. Damiani, who called Lawrence "a very articulate spokesman for various causes."

Damiani praised Lawrence for his "non-biased" approach to dealing with issues.

"He was a very intelligent man, and was never conscious of race in making his decisions."

At his Carver Street home last night, friends, relatives and church members grieved the untimely death of the man they had looked up to as a leader.

"He was an example of hard work and decency," a family friend said.

In his work as city housing manager and even before he joined the housing authority in 1979, Lawrence had dedicated many years to helping provide housing

See LAWRENCE, page 2

82

Obituaries

Lawrence will be buried Sunday

James W. Lawrence, 69, of 115 Carver Ave., died Wednesday in Louise Obici Memorial Hospital as the result of an automobile accident. A native of Nansemond County, he was the husband of Lucretia Lawrence, and son of the late Charlie Lawrence and Leila H. Scott.

He was employed at the Suffolk Redevelopment and Housing Authority, and had retired from the Norfolk Naval Shipyard after 30 years.

A graduate of Booker T. Washington High School, he also attended West Virginia State College, the Pearl Harbor Training School in Honolulu, Hawaii, and the Eastern School of Electricity in New York.

He was manager of Cypress Manor, Parker-Riddick and Hoffler Apartments in Suffolk. Lawrence was a member of Oak Grove Baptist Church and a veteran of the Air Force.

Besides his wife, survivors include two daughters, Mrs. Judy Chapman and Alisa Chapman, both of Suffolk; four sisters, Carrie B. Lawrence and Mrs. Ora V. Wells, both of Suffolk, and Mrs. Gracie A. Newby and Mrs. Frances M. Jones, both of New York City; one brother, John H. Lawrence; and five grandchildren.

The funeral will be conducted Sunday at 1 p.m. in Oak Grove Baptist Church by the pastor, Rev. Anthony Copeland. Burial will be in Carver Memorial Cemetery. Crocker Funeral Home in charge of arrangements.

James W. Lawrence

—Forum—————

Our view

A home for the homeless

With the death of Suffolk civic activist James W. Lawrence last week, Suffolk got a potential name for a potential project.

What better designation can there be than the James W. Lawrence Shelter for the Homeless?

At the time of his death in a car crash, Mr. Lawrence was seeking a seat on City Council, there to better foster one of his dreams—a home for the homeless. Mr. Lawrence, who was a housing manager for the Suffolk Redevelopment and Housing Authority, has long pushed the idea of providing a roof for those made temporarily homeless by eviction, an abusive spouse or other unhappy circumstances. It was a part of his overall view that a lot needs to be done in Suffolk to provide people with proper housing, despite all that has already been done.

With so many vacant buildings in Suffolk, Mr. Lawrence reasoned, it's a shame that one cannot be turned into a temporary home.

Gratifyingly, the city this year had already begun taking a hard look at the problem. City Manager John L. Rowe Jr. told Council in January that there are public and private resources geared to providing emergency housing for one or two nights, and also subsidized housing to provide long-term shelter. But there is little to offer individuals or families who may be down and out for an in between period of a week or two. Typical is the evicted or burned-out family in need of a roof while they hunt new shelter.

In some Virginia cities, private organizations have stepped in, operating homes which provide emergency shelter for periods of up to two weeks. Operational expenses include a full-time director, and these groups set financial assistance from local governments, United Ways and fundraising of their own.

Suffolk is a city of 50,000. It would seem such a population would generate a steady need for emergency housing. However, studies can and should be undertaken to determine the scope of the need and financial feasibility of a shelter.

This might be one of the first functions of a Suffolk Advisory Board on the Homeless which City Council created by resolution on March 6. The board is to have membership of up to 15, and Council is now seeking nominations.

There's a good chance that one of James Lawrence's dreams may become a reality.

Officer of the year

They've really got Det. J.J. Marx in a good spot at the Suffolk Police Department. A man extremely dedicated to, and enthusiastic about, his profession, Det. Marx's duties include seeking out and signing up new recruits for a job in which the detective's traits are all important.

The Suffolk Kiwanis Club last week, together with his fellow officers and superiors, recognized Det. Marx last week by naming him Police Officer of the Year. From all reports, it was a well-earned designation. Det. Marx, a 10-year veteran of the force, is a big believer in crime prevention; that type of police work is often less obvious, but stopping a crime before it happens is the ultimate in police work.

Congratulations to Det. Marx, and to the Kiwanians for their 10-year program of calling attention to good police officers through their annual award.

Lawrence group backs Goodman for council seat

By JOHN RAILEY
NEWS-HERALD REPORTER

The committee which once hoped to see the late James W. Lawrence elected as the Cypress Borough representative on City Council has announced its support of William H. Goodman.

In the statement, the committee said that the 47-year-old air traffic controller would represent the city in an "excellent manner," carrying on many of the ideals Lawrence represented.

Lawrence, a 69-year-old housing manager, was killed in a traffic accident last month.

According to the letter, the committee feels Goodman would stand for better education, open lines of communication with constituents, appoint "responsible people" as board members, and support "better recreation for his people."

A past president of the East Suffolk Gardens Civic League, Goodman established his candidacy for the position earlier this year.

One of four blacks in the city council race, Goodman is vying for the Cypress Borough slot against incumbent Vice Mayor Ronald O. Hart, who is also black.

In the letter endorsing Goodman, the committee said that, while Hart

See GOODMAN, page 2

85

−Hart────────────

Continued from page 1

"I don't place people on boards who I think I can control," Hart responded, "I put on people who are bright and able to think for themselves and make decisions which I hope will be in the best interest of the city. I have never told any appointee that they have to vote the same way I do."

Hart said Holland "has voted her conviction, and she is willing to talk to any group who wants to talk to her about the school issue."

Hart said, "I know there's one person from that group who is against me simply because of Mrs. Holland," but said, "I think Lula's doing a fine job."

Mrs. Holland was not available yesterday to respond to the charges by the committee.

Another allegation by the Lawrence group suggested Hart does not get along with other members of City Council.

Mayor Andrew B. Damiani said Tuesday he would not comment specifically on Hart, but said, "This council has gotten along extremely well in the past, and I think we communicate very well with each other as a group."

Hart said the committee's statements were unfounded, and said, "I do not know of any poor relationship that exists between council and myself, and I have no no idea where they got that information."

The vice mayor also said a charge that he had done nothing to get sewage and water extensions into the Cypress area was "one of the most ridiculous comments made in the statement."

Hart said, "Everyone can see the progress being made in this area. We still have a long way to go, but we're definitely getting there."

Parker-Riddick Apartments
in Suffolk, VA

Lawrence
Lauds Media

"I would like to publicly commend the Suffolk News-Herald and Radio Station WLPM for their efforts in trying to get some action started on the local water situation," James W. Lawrence of Nansemond County said in a statement issued last night. Lawrence has indicated he may run for the Nansemond County Board of Supervisors from the Cypress Magisterial District opposing Supervisor Moses A. Riddick Jr.

"There is little doubt that an informed citizenry in due time will bring about some action, and certainly the News-Herald and WLPM are to be lauded for bringing this issue before the people for consideration," Lawrence said.

His statement continues, "For many years I have been critical of the water situation between the City of Portsmouth and Nansemond County. It has severely hindered progress in the city-county area and will continue to hinder the orderly future progress of Suffolk and Nansemond County.

"It is my firm belief tha

(Continued on Page 8)

Installation

Chuckatuck-Hobson Branch of NAACP will hold their installation of officers Sunday at 4 p.m. at Diamond Grove Fellowship Hall, Sandy Bottom. Mr. James W. Lawrence will be the speaker. The public is invited.

Ex-Mayor Comments On Lawrence's Plan

Richard L. Woodward Jr., a former Mayor and City Councilman in the City of Suffolk and past president of the Tidewater Virginia Development Council, issued a statement this morning concerning proposals made last week by James W. Lawrence. Lawrence is considering the possibility of running for the Nansemond County Board of Supervisors.

Woodward's full statement follows:

"I have read, in your paper, some of the proposals regarding Nansemond County made by Mr. James W. Lawrence. I assume he is a resident of the County, and to his credit, it is evident he has given some thought to the county's problems and is seeking a solution.

"Unfortunately, some of his proposals are statutorily interdicted. For instance, the matter of taxing the water facilities of Portsmouth and Norfolk was brought before the courts during the tenure of Chas. B. Godwin Jr., Commonwealth Attorney. "It failed."

"As I remember it, one political subdivision cannot tax the property of another political subdivision. Suffolk, for instance, cannot tax the clerk's office nor the Court House of Nansemond County even though they are in the confines of the City.

"It has been intimated that he may run against Moses A. Riddick, Jr., for Supervisor. Before he decides to do so, he had better take a long hard look at his chances.

"My reason for saying this is that Mr. Riddick, from what I can read of his record, has made one of the best members of this Board in recent years.

"Due to the majority Negro population in the county, he possesses a keener insight into their needs. Because of this, he has brought to the attention of the Board and worked for a consummation of improvements that remained unattended for too many years. He also worked hard for the recent redevelopment proposal.

"Mr. Lawrence opposed the joint effort of the City and County for redevelopment and improvement of bad sanitary and housing conditions in the county, on the false premise that the city had the best of the joint agreement. Just the opposite was true because the City undertook to improve considerably more of the blighted area than did the county.

"He stated, if I remember correctly, what his proposals, recently written, implied, that he had reversed his thoughts on this subject. He also advocated the merger of the city and county. This is neither practical, feasible nor financially possible.

"In my opinion, the time has now arrived when the city should clean up its own blighted areas and let the county clean up theirs. In following this procedure the people of the county will realize that they rejected what would have redounded to their own best interest, and a tremendous saving in their future economy."

Brothers Parting Company

Two Suffolk brothers will bid their family adieu this week as they leave for much-separated parts of the world to serve with the U.S. Army. Jimmie Lee Benton, right, left here today (Wednesday) for a tour of duty at Stuttgart, Germany. His brother, John E., will be leaving Tuesday for duty in Vietnam. They are sons of Mr. and Mrs. A. L. Benton of 3077 Old Norfolk Rd.

For Improvement of Conditions In County

James Lawrence Offers 14-Point Plan

Minimum Housing

Nansemond County desperately needs a minimum Housing ordinance to insure that homes now being built and to be built in the future will meet a certain standard and will not contribute to our present or same future slum condition.

Improving Existing Property

Because of the condition of much of the existing housing in the County, immediate steps should be taken toward improvement - a certain minimum standard should be set, and the owners be given a reasonable length of time to comply. This should apply to all sub-standard property including rental housing - such a program would work only a minimum of hardship because there are several methods of financing available: (1) Private money (2) Home improvement loans at banks, building & loan associations, credit unions, F. H. A. (3) A plan backed by the Federal Government whereby the aged, or persons from low income families may obtain low interest long time loans for home improvements. The plan should be drawn so as to make allowances for extreme hardship cases.

Water Control Board

Millions of gallons of water are constantly being drawn from the water sheds of Nansemond County over which the county has absolutely no control. Water is a valuable natural resource without which man could not long exist - Nansemond was endowed by nature with a plentiful supply, however other's control it, profit from it and could even deny it's use to County residents, should they so desire - this is an intolerable situation - a water control board should be set up and empowered to protect the interests of county residents.

Water Tax

The water business is the largest business owned by the city of Portsmouth, each year they do business in the millions of dollars - the city of Norfolk does a big water business, supplying themselves and selling to others, they recently need it as a bargaining point in negotiations with the city of Virginia Beach. It just does not strike me as good business when others can gain so much from something that belongs to us. True they own the land on which the pumps are located and much of the surrounding properties but water streams do not adhere to property boundary lines, and as a result water is being pumped from all over the county, A County Tax should be imposed on each million gallons ex-

tracted in Nansemond County and the proceeds used to help pay the cost of a sewage disposal plant.

Water Contract

Public utilities all over the nation and in almost every instance, pay for their own transmission lines - in the case of Power and Gas Companies they even affix their lines to the residence's being served - strange indeed is the water contract between Nansemond County and the city of Portsmouth, we must buy the lines and deed them to the Portsmouth Water Company. Then we must pay a fee to tap the lines we paid for before we can use the water extracted from the lakes located in our county. This legal robbery of Nansemond County Tax payers has been too long tolerated. Negotiations on a new water contract should be begun immediately and the thousands of dollars now being donated to the Portsmouth economy yearly, would go a long way toward paying for the county

Sewage Disposal Plant

The State & Federal Governments realizing the tremendous cost of sewage disposal and the hardship on a community such as ours and realizing the great need for such facilities, have set aside huge sums of money to aid in the construction of sewage disposal plants, Nansemond County with a little planning could well afford to have sewage disposal in the thickly populated areas. This could be accomplished with the proper use of local, state and federal funds and would not require a major tax raise.

Continued Tomorrow.

More Points In Lawrence's 13-Point Plan Are Offered

In yesterday's News-Herald James Lawrence, a county citizen who says he is considering running for a position on the Board of Supervisors, presented the first six points in a 13-point program he proposes for the betterment of the county. The last seven of his points follow today.

SEWAGE USE TAX

To dispel any opposition to the sewage disposal plant a "use tax" could be imposed, and the people actually using the facilities would pay the county's part of the cost. State and Federal money plus the suggested reforms would keep the cost to a bare minimum and put this much needed service within the reach of everyone.

ESTABLISH: BUILDING, PLUMBING AND WIRING INSPECTIONS

The sad story of run down and collapsing buildings, frequent electrical fires and some poor sanitary conditions is the direct result of negligence on the part of the present and past governing body's of this county — many of the homes that comprise the slum area's today, were slums when they were built. There were no laws to protect the home buyer from shoddy workmanship on the part of the builder, there were no laws to protect him from inferior work and materials in his wiring and plumbing. There are still no laws to protect him. There is still nothing on the books to restrain the greedy, get-rich-quick type of person who builds houses for rent and is only interested in collecting the weekly rent which is usually twice as much as the property is worth, this is probably the greatest single contributer to the county's present blighted condition — to set the record straight this is not a blanket indictment of the people who offer houses for rent. I know of several who take much personal pride in the condition of houses they offer for rent. Building, wiring and plumbing inspections should be started immediately and rigidly enforced.

MUDDY ROADS

The pace that muddy impassable roads in the county are being eliminated is far too slow, there are not many things imaginable that add more to slum conditions, not many things contribute more to unsanitary living conditions, and causes a larger loss of incentive among the people who must live on them, until this problem is solved the whole problem of slum clearance is hopeless. All the tax payer, can expect from the board is a promise that they will refer the matter to the state highway department which in turn promptly informs you that there is no money available for improvements in your area. Whenever improvements are made it is generally done on a partisan basis. It is inconceivable that in these modern times, that people in Nansemond County must live on roads that are actually in worse shape than when they were Indian trails.

SUNDAY BEER SALES

There have many things been said about the controversial ban on the sale of beer on Sunday. The Board of Supervisors mulled over the issue several times without reaching a decision. It was finally tabled, which is a polite way of saying it was thrown in the waste basket. Personally I believe the members of the board should stand up and be counted on any issue regardless of how controversial it might be. If the board was unable to reach a decision, then they should have it placed on the ballot and let the people decide for themselves.

PEST CONTROL

Study the cost of mosquito and rat control. These pest are biproducts of slums and are disease carriers.

FIRE PROTECTION

Study our present fire protection with a view toward establishing sub station (or) stations as required to provide reasonable fire protection for county residents

MERGER

Appoint a special committee to study in detail with a city counter-part in detail the feasibility of merger the city still needs land for expansion and the county still needs protection from a Portsmouth take over of one of its vital areas, there are numerous reasons for seeking merger by both the city and county.

Good Afternoon

By THE ASSOCIATED PRESS

Viet Cong battalions are being broken up into small units for a renewal of guerrilla war, U.S. intelligence reports indicate.

Harrison Salisbury, who visited North Vietnam, says in an interview restrictions put on him were "mild considering that this is a country engaged in a very tough war."

Premier Chou En-lai is reported engaged in an effort to mediate the costly struggle between Mao Tse-tung and Liu Shao-chi, president of Red China.

Lester G. Maddox appeals for unity and support after being elected governor of Georgia by the legislature.

KKK Is Held

Peace Threat

HALIFAX AP — The Halifax County Ministerial Association, in a pair of resolutions released this week, has condemned the Ku Klux Klan as "a real threat to the peace, harmony and well-being" of the county.

Is Willing to Debate Plan, Lawrence Says

James W. Lawrence today answered comments published yesterday from Richard L. Woodward Jr., and challenged Woodward to a debate on proposals Lawrence made last week for Nansemond County.

Lawrence proposed 13 points last week he considered vital to the county, after revealing the possibility that he might run for the Board of Supervisors. Woodward, a former Mayor of Suffolk, challenged several of the points made by Lawrence.

The statement issued today by Lawrence follows.

"I have the utmost respect for both Mr. Richard L. Woodward Jr. and his opinions concerning what is best for Nansemond County. I am sure he has the interests of Suffolk and Nansemond County at heart, and due to his wide experience possesses some very intelligent opinions.

"However, I must take issue with him on some of the points raised in his recent statement critical of the 13 point program I have proposed for the County. To begin with my proposal contained 13 points and if Mr. Woodward found fault with only one of the 13 points this gives me a pretty good batting average, one out of 13 is pretty good in any league.

"I have already taken some of your advice I took several long hard looks at my chances in the supervisor's race as have many other voters in my district. Hence my decision to make an announcement of my intentions through these newspaper colums within the next two weeks.

"As to your statement regarding Mr. Riddick, (Supervisor Moses A. Riddick Jr.)

I will make no comment at this time. If and when I enter the race will be time enough to discuss his record with the voters.

"I have not reversed my thoughts concerning the urban renewal plan offered to the voters in November, I opposed it then, I oppose it now and will oppose it in the future if

a similar package is offered. I considered it a county giveaway then and my thoughts haven't changed. As to whether the proposal was good or bad, is a matter of opinion, you have your's and surely I am entitled to mine.

"I would be only too glad to debate the merits and demerits of the proposal in a public Continued On Page 10

Turner Named On Study Commission

W. Lovell Turner, general superintendent of Nansemond County Schools, has accepted an appointment to the governor's study commission on vocational rehabilitation.

As a member of the commission, he will help provide over - all leadership and guidance in a state-wide study of vocational rehabilitation needs in Virginia, and to recommend a plan of action.

Turner has been with the Nansemond County School System since 1939. For 27 years he was principal of East Suffolk High School. After one year as principal of John F. Kennedy High School, he became general superintendent in 1966. Much of his time is now devoted to the school drop-out problem.

A native of Talladega, Ala., he finished grammar and high school in Gary, Ind. With a major in education and a minor in sociology, he received from Howard University, Washington, D.C., his BA degree in 1929 and his masters in 1930.

Then came graduate work at New York University and Hampton Institute.

Prior to Suffolk, he taught at Claflin University, Orangeburg, S.C.; Allen University, Columbia, S.C.; and St. Phillips Junior College, San Antonio, Texas.

Coming to this area in 1935 he first taught at the Nansemond Collegiate Institute.

W. LOVELL TURNER
...appointed

James Lawrence **Not Running**

"After giving long and studious thought to the request of numerous friends and voters of the Cypress District, I have decided not to offer for the Board of Supervisors race at this time," said James W. Lawrence.

"My reasons for declining to run in the up coming elections are several and varied."

Lawrence them listed the following:

"I believe that no supervisor will be effective unless he has the confidence of the people he is to represent, like-wise I believe that a supervisor should truly represent all of the people of his district, and not just a chosen few who would seek to dictate to the majority.

"I feel that objectives and endorsements should be made in open public meetings and that personal gain should not be a factor in determining those objectives and endorsements."

"Because internal dissension can serve only to divide and render any supervisor ineffective, I have decided to diligently seek these reforms within the present framework, failing in these efforts, I shall then support the candidates whom in my opinion will do most for the district and the county.

"Because I know it is impossible for me or any other supervisor to live and raise a family on the $1,600 salary paid for the job, and realizing that I would have to have another job or source of revenue, it would be fool hardy to resign from my present position. The meager salary paid could not possibly sustain a supervisor.

"I believe that my present role of Constructive Critic of the board will add greatly to the progress of Nansemond County and its people at heart, and will endeavor at all times to work for those interests."

On urban renewal Lawrence said: "If the same urban renewal package is again offered to the voters, I will vigorously oppose and organize opposition against it. However; if a plan is offered that is equitable to both the city and county, it will receive my firm support."

"I believe that the ultimate answer to City-County problems is merger, and since no detailed study has been made of merger possibilities despite the fact that thousands of dollars were spent on the redevelopment proposal, leads me to believe there is a skeleton in the closet."

"Again many thanks to my friends and supporters who urged me to make the race, am truly sorry that I cannot answer your request in the affirmative, however; this does not close the door to some future race."

JAMES W. LAWRENCE
...not candidate

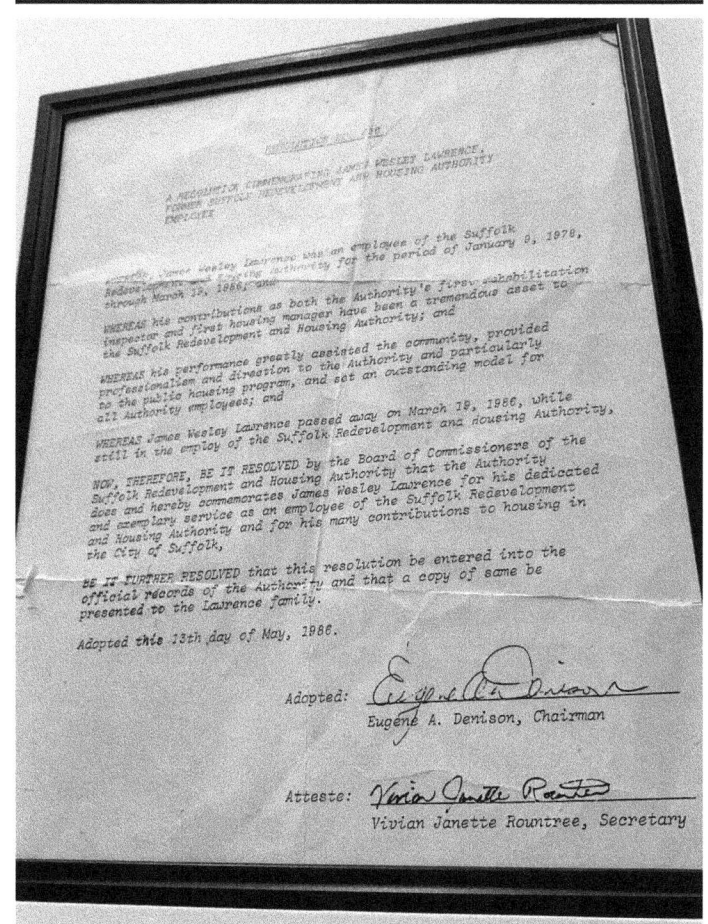

Cypress Manor Beautification Efforts Are Praised

BY CAROLE MAGUIRE

Residents of Cypress Manor received praise for their unanimous efforts towards beautification of their neighborhood Friday afternoon as city officials toured the area and admired their work.

Housing manager ... conducted the tour along with Suffolk Redevelopment and Housing Authority Director L. Judson Barrett.

... called attention to the fact that the persons living there have made an attempt to improve their surroundings by planting grass, shrubs and flowers.

The apartment buildings are modern looking and ... said the residents often work outside until late into the evening working at their yards.

He said, "People thought this would be another slum, and look around and see what the people have done."

A prize of $50 was offered for the building judged by the touring group to have the nicest yards. Building one won that honor with newly planted and trimmed grass, marigold borders and neat shrubbery. Six families will split the money.

... said the public housing development has been able to accomplish a well-run neighborhood, with help from city officials including the housing authority.

Barrett said it was all possible because the city-owned [?] unit development is staffed with a certified housing manager ... with counselors and with many people, "who work with Mr ... and help him."

He said many of the persons who moved to Cypress Manor "had no idea of what it was like to have an indoor bathroom."

Lawrence, obviously proud, called attention to the lights that burn on the buildings at night. They're amber and when they're all lit up at night you never saw a night so beautiful.

The Mayor, J.W. Nelms Jr, commended ... for a "good job." On the tour Nelms praised several residents for their hard work. "An asset to the city."

... noted a low crime rate in the Cypress Manor development. He said kids fight sometimes but the fights are soon broken up.

Del Lt R.C. Law said the management in that neighborhood has been helpful to police and are "working on making Cypress Manor a decent place for people to live."

Barrett told Nelms that housing of friends from Portsmouth were challenged to come to Suffolk to see the neighborhood and how well-kept it is. "We've had 99.5 percent participation. These people have a different outlook on life than they had before. It shows that most housing can change people." Lawrence said, and is proud positive that public housing can work.

Nelms asked why other housing developments haven't been able to accomplish what Cypress Manor has and he asked what could be done in the future to insure like results.

He was told that there is no control in private developments as there is in public housing.

... discussed with City Manager G. Robert House Jr. what he called a lack of a playing area large enough for such games as baseball. Barrett said there wasn't enough land available at this time to expand for a large play area.

There is an area for basketball and at least two play areas with equipment for young children. The playgrounds are supervised.

The tour included many single story homes including one on Eagle Square. Mr. and Mrs. Otis Smith said they are enjoying their home. They came from the Hollywood section where Mrs. Smith said they had no hot water facilities.

Lawrence, who is certified as a housing manager with the National Association of Housing and Redevelopment Authority Officials, satisfied some of the six families in building one that their front yards had received the first place prize.

Other city officials on the tour where Tom Underwood, assistant city manager; Pat Cofield and Miles Starfish, staff members with the city manager; ... Varalla, director of community development and Bert Beasley, assistant city attorney.

Among some of the winners congratulated by L. Judson Barrett, ... and G. Robert House Jr., were Mrs. Wanda Britt, William Britt, Sandra K. Davis in her grandmother's arms, Vonnie Davis and Jeremiah Davis; Beverly Brown and Juanita Brown. All live in building one and received a prize of $50 for first place in a yard judging contest.

Lawrence Certified As Housing Manager

The manager of Suffolk's first city-owned public housing project has been certified by a national organization as a public housing manager.

James W. Lawrence, manager of Cypress Manor, received the certification from the National Association of Housing and Redevelopment Officials (NAHRO) after successfully completing an eight-month training period and "rigorous" examinations.

Suffolk's Redevelopment and Housing Authority executive director, L. Judson Barrett, Wednesday presented Lawrence with his NAHRO certificate in a ceremony at Cypress Manor.

Barrett told the press Lawrence was one of only eight or nine public housing project managers in Virginia to receive the NAHRO certificate.

The U.S. Department of Housing and Urban Development has begun requiring some housing project managers to complete the NAHRO course.

... city-owned housing project, Parker-Riddick Village, will also be managed by Lawrence.

Cypress Manor manager James W. Lawrence, right received his official certification as a public housing project manager in a ceremony Wednesday. Suffolk's Redevelopment and Housing Authority executive director, L. Judson Barrett, left, presented him with the certificate.

94

Your view

Candidate Lawrence extolled by daughter

I am writing to you simply to air my opinion concerning the upcoming City Council election. It is my belief that God has given each of us something to do.

There is a need in my borough (Cypress) as well as the entire city of Suffolk for positive action. We have heard great promises as to how our community will improve. I have yet to witness many of these promises becoming realities. This can only be due to one of two things: the lack of good leadership or the lack of our so-called leaders' ability to take a stand. I am a firm believer that a person must stand up for something or fall for anything. I am focusing my opinions mainly on two candidates, Mr. _____ _____ and Vice Mayor Ronald Hart. I feel that I am justified in stating that, as a teacher, Mr. Hart is one of the finest and as a councilman, the same would apply to Mr. _____ _____.

Mr. _____ _____ has been a leader in our community for as long as I can remember. He has done great things, not only for this borough but for the city as a whole. During the time that Mr. Hart was grading papers, Mr. _____ _____ was doing other great things. He was one of the people responsible for bringing the late Rev. Martin Luther King to Suffolk, obtaining Cypress Park in Hollywood, getting streets lights and paved streets in Oakdale; having gates installed at the railroad tracks on Capitol Street and many other great accomplishments, too numerous to mention in this letter.

It is my belief that Vice Mayor Hart has good intentions but that alone won't do. We need a man who can and who will follow through. A man who is not intimidated by those in higher positions. A man who sees what needs to be done and rolls up his sleeves. A man who will first seek the needs of his people through personal consultations and then set goals, relentlessly following through until those goals are met. A man who is not prejudiced against race, gender or social standing but is a firm believer that everybody is somebody. A man who is absolutely against violence, but who is wholeheartedly for reasoning and fair play. A man who is aware of the importance of the needs and voices of the youth in our everchanging society. A man with experience enough to know how to set about obtaining goals, intelligent enough to know his limitations, secure enough to take a stand, wise enough to know what is beneficial to his constituents, bold enough to fight for what he believes in, educated to know the importance of a sound education and successful enough to know that, given a chance, a child brought up in poverty can surpass all obstacles and become what our city needs more of, good leaders and good followers as well.

"Why?", some may ask "has he decided to run now. For the income? For prestige? I think not. He has gone on record stating that if his present job as housing manager would be a conflict he would resign. He has already committed a sizeable portion of his salary, if elected, to a worthy cause. Prestige is not something sought after by the candidate, but rather something that is naturally applied to him, because of the greatness that he projects. There is no doubt in my mind that _____ _____ _____ is our man.

Judy Chapman,
Suffolk, Va.

Editor's Note: Mrs. Chapman is a daughter of Candidate _____ _____ _____.

Lawrence

Continued from page 1

for Suffolk's underprivileged.

"He was in such a jolly mood yesterday," said his daughter, Judy Chapman. "It's so untimely, but he accomplished so much in his life. He lived a rich, full life, and he worked until the day he died."

At 68, Lawrence had battled illness and injuries from another car accident in the last year. But his daughter, who lived with her father, said he was feeling good: he was active and looking forward to the upcoming City Council elections.

Lawrence's death leaves two challengers – William H. Goodman and Wong-ya G. Jones – to vie for the Cypress borough seat held by Vice Mayor Ronald O. Hart.

During his run for council, Lawrence cited improvements in education and upgraded housing as a major goal, and also stressed the importance of developing a shelter to temporarily serve those without housing.

"The lack of a shelter for our homeless here in Suffolk borders on criminal negligence," Lawrence noted in January. "There are a number of old buildings here in the city which are not being used for a thing, and that makes no sense at all when there are people who need shelter."

When Lawrence announced his candidacy Jan. 4, he stressed his friendship with Hart and said, "I'm not running against anyone. I'm running for a position on City Council."

Hart said last night he and Lawrence had a close relationship, and called Lawrence "a very intelligent man who has been able to accomplish a lot. This community and this city should be so proud of him."

SOUR Sitting Back During Talks

By CAROLE MAGUIRE

The president of SOUR, the group formed to protest the drilling and pumping of wells in Driver, said today his organization is being quiet lately because Tidewater cities are doing what SOUR has been asking them to do all along — negotiating.

James W. Lawrence said his group is laying low because, "we don't want to muddy the water. You don't browbeat people when they are doing what you asked them to do. But if things turn out unfavorably, we will be right back in the middle."

Last fall, SOUR members attended a Norfolk City Council meeting and asked that body to sit down with Suffolk officials and work out solutions to what has become a legal battle over use and control of groundwater.

"Litigation didn't produce any water," Lawrence said. "It looks like something might come out of this," he added, referring to negotiations which have been taking place between cities and counties with ample supplies and with water-poor communities to the east.

Norfolk has agreed in principle to allow Virginia Beach to negotiate for the purchase of water from western cities and counties. They have not, however, formalized a contract amendment with Virginia Beach which specifies the resort city can be supplied water only from Norfolk.

But Norfolk Mayor Vincent Thomas said the amendment will be formalized. Last Thursday, at a meeting of the Southeastern Public Service Authority of Virginia, he said there has never been any problem with allowing Virginia Beach to get its water elsewhere during the drought emergency.

Norfolk and Suffolk lawyers have been talking about several concessions Norfolk would like to have before granting that permission to Virginia Beach.

Lawrence says everyone can come out a winner if Suffolk agrees with Virginia Beach in contract negotiations related to an approximate 8 million gallons a day (mgd) flowing from this city to the resort city through Norfolk lines and treatment facilities.

"Some concessions would be in order," he said, like allowing Norfolk to repair existing transmission lines which are known to leak. But, he said, Norfolk should be required to take down the existing pipes connecting the western reservoir system with Norfolk if Norfolk is allowed to replace the old line with a new one.

Concerning the pump improvement program by Norfolk here, Lawrence felt that should be allowed to continue as long as Norfolk's pumpage is monitored and restricted. "If Norfolk does this work and new pumps or lines make increased capacity, Norfolk could pump untold millions of gallons out."

STOP services reach out to community

By JUDY CHAPMAN
CORRESPONDENT
934-0657

The STOP Community Service Center is continuing to expand its services to the community.

They are meeting emergency needs with food, clothing, furniture, and other essentials needed by many families.

In addition to these needs, assistance is given to people needing help in completing various forms such as birth certificate applications, name changes, and free lunch forms.

For the past two weeks, Ruby Walden, STOP's coordinator of community services for the cities of Suffolk, Franklin, Isley of Wight, and Southampton counties, has spent a great deal of time working with the Cypress Community League and the Suffolk branch of the N.A.A.C.P. in coordinating a city-wide effort to increase voter registration.

Through this effort, 18 volunteers have been qualified to serve as alternating dates. More than 100 new voters were added to the books during a full day's effort at Suffolk's armory recently.

East Suffolk Complex will be opened for registration each day until October 3 from 10 a.m. to 4 p.m. for voter registration.

"We feel being a registered voter is every individual's right, duty and privilege, and it should be utilized," says Walden.

The STOP Community Service Programs recently responded to a request made by James W. Lawrence, manager of Cypress Manor and Parker-Riddick Apartments, and conducted a workshop on home management and home care for residents who are soon to be transferred to the Hoffler Apartments.

All residents will be required to attend this type of workshop in the future before occupying these apartments.

Lawrence felt an introduction to the use and care of the utilities and facilities will help to make the transition from one location to another much easier.

Walden spoke to the group about the various services available to them in emergencies through the STOP program. She emphasized the importance of maintaining a clean, safe home.

"We must take good care of what we have and take pride in keeping it as attractive and serviceable as possible," said Walden.

Charlene Colter, extension home economist, made the presentation on "home care," using slides, showing in detail the best methods to use in the cleaning of all the equipment in the apartments, stressing cleaning supplies need not be expensive. Follow up sessions are scheduled bimonthly.

The Headstart Program is open at this time with a 100 percent enrollment.

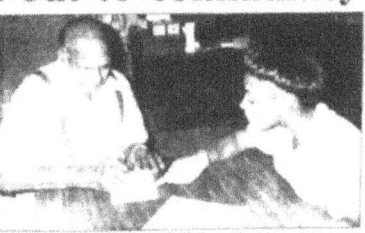

Volunteer registrar helps a Suffolk resident in registering to vote.

Hill Underwood
Funeral Home

SERVICE WITH DIGNITY
SINCE 1891

H.M. UNDERWOOD
PRESIDENT

Corner Washington and Wellons Sts.
Phone 539-3486

Million

Our view

Signal is coming, but when?

As a result of a traffic count, the Virginia Department of Highways and Transportation has concluded that a traffic signal is needed and will be installed at Portsmouth Boulevard and Suburban Drive – the intersection where City Council candidate James W. Lawrence, lost his life in a two-car crash March 19.

But, as a News-Herald story reported Tuesday, that doesn't mean a light will be installed anytime soon. The project must be put on a list and await its turn. It could be next year, or it could be years, an official said.

The Highway Department has some pretty strict criteria which must be met before a traffic signal can be installed. The fact that someone was killed at a corner is not enough. The fact that motorists perceive an intersection as hazardous is not enough. Many motorists believe traffic signals are cure alls, and if the department heeded each request, there'd

be a traffic signal at almost every crossing.

On the contrary, when the department decides a signal is warranted, you can count on it that the potential hazard has been deemed great.

At Portsmouth and Suburban, the department determined that traffic on Portsmouth was so heavy that traffic on Suburban "suffers excessive delay or hazard in entering or crossing the major street." To fall within this criteria, one of 11 under which traffic signal installations can be approved, Portsmouth met the requirement of having a traffic count of at least 630 vehicles per hour, and Suburban, as the minor street, of at least 53 per hour.

Something is wrong, however, when an "excessive hazard" is identified, and nothing can be done about it for months or years. Traffic signals don't come cheap – you can sink $35,000 or much more into one installation – but

something needs to be done immediately about an identified excessive danger.

The Highway Department, of course, must work within its budget, which consists of monies for maintenance of existing roads and construction of new roads. When it comes to priorities for spending existing monies, however, one would think that unsafe roads would be made safe before new roads are built.

The shortage of money to meet identified traffic signal needs is but one example of the crying need to pump new money – vast amounts of it – into Virginia's highway system. Virginia not only needs to maintain the safety of existing roads, but to have funds for pressing new construction. That need will be addressed Sept. 15 when the General Assembly meets in special session to consider the financing of a $10 billion transportation program.

Your view

Sympathy extended to Lawrence family

The Lawrence family has my sincere sympathy.

Mr. James Lawrence and I were working together as members of the Neighborhood Advisory Council for the STOP organization here in Suffolk.

He has been known to me as a friend to my family since 1952.

I have always admired and respected his leadership as he sought to better living conditions for the citizens of Suffolk.

The citizens of Suffolk have suffered a great loss in the passing of Mr. James Lawrence Thursday, March 19, 1986.

Im am truly sorry and with God's help we will fulfill his mission in the May elections.

William H. Goodman,
City Council candidate,
Cypress borough

CHAPTER FIFTEEN
THE THINGS THE WORLD DID NOT SEE

My dad was not a seeker of attention, accolades, or applause. He was a 100% authentic human being who had a heart of gold. As mentioned in my letter to the City Council, he was a born humanitarian. On countless occasions, after finding out about a hungry family, he would either take me or the family to Belo's, a grocery store located on Constance Rd. in Suffolk, to fill cabinets, pantries and refrigerators. He would not only shop for the basics and staples; we would go over to the bread store to purchase treats. He was not only a competent man; he was a compassionate man as well, and his benevolence went beyond supplying the need. He loved accommodating some of their desires. He treated the families as if they were his own. It literally took his appetite when he was aware of someone else's hunger.

Whenever my dad saw any sort of need, it became his mission

to do all he could to supply whatever he could. His giving heart led some to believe he was a rich man, and he was, in every way that mattered.

I remember once when he was planning to adopt a son named Leroy. Everything was being prepared for him to become a part of our household until the day Daddy looked out of the window when he heard me cry. There was Leroy in the front yard twisting my arm as hard as he could. I don't have to tell you how the tentative adoption played out after that. That was the absolute wrong thing for Leroy to do.

There was also a case where a young boy named Casey was shot by his uncle. I don't know how my dad found out about him, but he immediately took action. He was there with him for the duration of his hospital stay and brought him home until he had completely recovered. I can't remember what happened after that, but I know for sure that Daddy stayed connected to him as long as he was needed.

Daddy had a special love for senior citizens. Whether the need was financial, a leaky roof, a yard full of leaves, a stove in need of coal or chopped wood, a medical emergency, needed shelter, food, loneliness, or just a positive outlook, he made himself available. He was willing to make whatever sacrifices necessary. He wasn't a pope, preacher, bishop, priest, cardinal, deacon, elder, archbishop, pastor, clergy or chaplain, but he was most assuredly, a man of God. He never sought to be served; his desire was to serve. A man after God's own heart.

My mother told me about an elderly neighbor in our neighborhood who had her grandchildren living with her. One day, as the construction workers were at our home working and throwing away boards that they didn't need, the elderly lady's grandchildren were picking them up to take them home to make a fire in their wood stove. When my dad was made aware of what they were doing, he ordered a truckload of firewood to be delivered to their home. Daddy's life was all about servitude and giving freely to others.

I have recordings of my mom sharing those memories. I am beyond blessed that my mom is still here as of this writing, at ninety-six years old. I pray that upcoming generations to come get to see and hear the foundation of their existence.

The thing that gives my heart so much joy is that most of the wonderful actions of kindness he performed, he preferred for them to be discreetly between God, him and the recipient. I refer to them as "actions of kindness" rather than acts of kindness because too often, that's exactly what they are—acts or performances, if you will.

People have told me many stories about the way my dad extended his hands to help someone. Every time I hear one of the stories, it feels like a piece of my dad has come back to me. I wish there were words to describe the way I feel for my dad. The words escape me, yet I am trying to bring honor to his name and legacy. There was no one like him. I may not understand why he had to leave me that day, but I know that the work he did was purposeful, he fulfilled his calling, and God is pleased. I pray that I leave a strong legacy of faith, benevolence, and kindness, like my dad.

CHAPTER SIXTEEN

SPECIAL MEMORIES

I can't remember the details of my 50th birthday party but, some memories from my childhood are as fresh in my mind as if it was yesterday. I remember our barbecue pit in the backyard; Mama seasoned the hamburgers and Daddy grilled them. The backyard would be lit by the floodlight that hung over the outside of the kitchen window. I can't remember if we played music or not, but if we did, I'm sure Fats Domino and Nat King Cole were two of the singers.

One of my favorites was the outdoor movies. I remember being snuggled with my parents after Daddy went out to grab the speaker to put inside our window and to get popcorn. It was one of the best moments of my life. Even though I always went to sleep, I was with the two people who loved me most in the world.

I also loved riding back to New York and visiting with our family. I looked forward to stopping at Howard Johnson to grab a bite to eat, use the restroom, and check out the souvenirs. It became very familiar to me and one of my favorite parts of the trips. It did not matter whether it was a car ride or on the Greyhound bus.

I have precious memories of my mother cooking breakfast while Daddy was mowing the lawn. I still love the aroma of frying bacon and a freshly mowed lawn.

I used to love swinging on my swings in the backyard with my friends. Playing with Agnes, Diane, Synda, Diann, Priscilla and Lee Lee was the height of my day. Later the Barnes family moved in, and we had even more fun with Clara, Gloria, Brenda and Cynthia.

Speaking of the Barnes family, many were the days that I enjoyed eating the nice hot biscuits Ms. Marion used to make. I preferred eating beans and franks with Kool-Aid at their house than steak and potatoes with iced tea at mine. I always felt welcomed there. I was even the one who pierced everyone's ears.

I will never forget the day in kindergarten when I accidentally spilled my milk on Synda's dress. Her mom, Ms. Annie, was very upset, and she had words with Mama. They stopped speaking for a while, but Synda and I never stopped playing together. Sometimes we fought, but it never lasted long.

As teenagers, we decided to be in the talent show at John F. Kennedy High School. Synda, Diann and I had pink hip-hugger bell-bottom pants and wore black bodysuits. We practiced every day at my house and sang "Baby" by Carla Thomas that night. We just knew that we were superstars.

My dad always made sure that I had every possible thing to make me happy at my disposal. Synda was with me, one day, when I came home. There, sitting on a table in the living room, was a record player and some Beatles records. We exploded! We danced wildly around the room as we heard the words, "He loves you… yeah…yeah…yeah!"

One day, I fell in my cousin James Artis' yard and broke my arm; Ms. Rosa came out, told me to wiggle my fingers, and it was decided that my arm wasn't broken. However, I kept having pain in it, so Daddy took me to the doctors'. After the X-ray, they discovered that it had actually been broken and had begun mending out of place. They had to re-break the bone, put it back together properly, and put it in a cast.

There is a funny caveat—my friend, Barbara Skeeter and I got into a fight on the schoolyard. While I was punching with one arm, I was protecting the other. I wish that we had cell phones back then; that had to have been hilarious to watch. It probably would have gone viral.

I spent a lot of time at the Wright's house. Agnes was one of my favorite play pals. Before my dad added the garage, I could actually talk to her from our bathroom window. Our garage had a few transformations. First, it was turned into a dancehall for me, and then later, an apartment for Daddy, complete with living room, dining room, bedroom, bathroom and kitchen. Yes, it was that large.

As a single mom of four, and in order to provide me with some independence without a lot of responsibility, my dad allowed me to run the house. He decided to move to the garage where he made a very comfortable dwelling. It went from a garage to a dancehall to an apartment—that man seemed to have a solution for everything!

The memory of having dinner with our family in Saratoga causes me to chuckle even now; especially when I think about us being served something we didn't want to eat and hiding it behind a piece of furniture, deep freezer or whatever we could find. It is a wonder they never had roaches or mice. We used to have the best time playing records and dancing on the inside of the house or playing 123 red light, catching "Junie bugs" (lightning bugs) and attaching them to string, or eating pears from the pear tree in the backyard. Or fighting to lick the ice cream dasher after the homemade ice cream had been finished. 522 Brook Avenue was definitely an active home and was the beginning for many of our family members.

These memories came flooding back when I became a mother and needed my aunts to watch Allen and Nichole. My aunts were older, so all they did was sit on the porch, rocking back and forth. Allen and Nichole hated sitting on the porch swinging back and forth on that metal rocking long chair. They had the saddest faces because they knew, with the exception of using the bathroom and meals, they would be there all day. Daddy taught me the importance of choosing the right people to babysit my children. Someone who loved and protected them was top priority.

Looking back at these memories, I can understand myself more. People didn't "get me" as I came up; they didn't seem to understand my way of thinking and doing things. But I choose to reflect on the good memories. I see myself through my memories.

I see my dad and family. I choose to focus on what matters, rather than focusing on what doesn't. Memories matter. They keep us connected to our core selves. The memories helped me to survive.

CHAPTER SEVENTEEN
A NEW PERSPECTIVE

After conversations with my children, we arrived at the conclusion that my father and I followed the same course. We poured into people who not only didn't value us, but rather detested us—eventually rejected us. It sent chills through my body as I reflected on times I gave my all to someone who secretly hated me. Just like with my dad, too many times, we were a means to an end, which is why we were often frustrated.

On this journey of having my dad's legacy un-erased, some masks were removed. I entertained stories of how my father opened some doors and held them open to help someone who needed it. As I listened and reflected, I realized that once the door was opened, it was slammed in his face. He knowingly allowed it because his motives were pure, just as by example, he taught his daughter to do.

Many politicians lacked two attributes essential in gaining public favor. It stands to reason that they would seek these attributes in another individual and attach themselves; thus, dishonestly portraying honesty and integrity. This is the tick mentality. They suck the blood, and once filled to capacity, move on to another prey.

When you love someone as much as I love my dad, thinking of someone hating him is incomprehensible. I've come to realize, I am hated just as much by some. I was oblivious to it until Daddy's life was eliminated. It was once said that my dad was "too intelligent and had too much money to be a black man." I remember somewhat of the same thing being said to me. I was "too dark to have little lips and curly hair." Oh! And I also had legs like a "white" girl. I can't make this stuff up! It's crazy!

I know for sure that this wasn't the world God had in mind when He created it, and I can see Him in the spirit, looking down and shaking His head. It must be something to watch, seeing His children giving themselves away in honor of Who He is, of making sacrifices that cause deficits in their own lives, trying to pour new wine into old wineskins all while trying to survive.

Sometimes, I feel like the Garden of Eden is just around the corner from me. It's beautiful and full of life; it has everything we need to live a fruitful life, yet, sitting there on a limb of the tree of knowledge of good and evil is a demonic agenda. The fruit looks delicious; it's filled with pats on the back, kisses on the cheeks and kudos, but once you take a bite, you find worms—snakes if you will.

The devil won't be found wearing horns and flaming red jumpsuits; that's how he gets you. His wardrobe has changed to flattery and a membership invitation to the good old boys' club. It's actually sickening thinking about the time some people invest in bringing someone to their knees. However, what they don't realize is that they have empowered their victim because they have positioned him or her for battle! It all begins on our knees.

God keeps us going by giving us a foretaste of divine glory—a preview of what is to come. If He laid out His Plan for us with the details, we would cower in the trenches of fear because we would be privy to every hiccup, every bump in the road, every incline, every decline, every wall, every detour and every mountain. We would change lanes or look for exits. We would make U-turns and head right back into the mess He was delivering us from. God lays out His Plan incrementally because He knows the dose we can handle. That is why it is detrimental moving before He says, "Move" or speaking when He says, "Be quiet" or going from point A to point Z when He says, "Be still."

I believe Daddy lived a life of hearing from God even though he wasn't in church every Sunday. Church was "in" him every day. As aforementioned, his last Sunday on earth was in church, and after joining, his last Monday was spent being a blessing to the household of faith. God knew that he wasn't going to be there for years, warming the pews. He accepted Daddy's plea for forgiveness, received him back into the fold, expeditiously used him within seventy-two hours to serve his fellowman before delivering him from a body of death into a marvelous eternity. That's the God I serve!

CHAPTER EIGHTEEN

DADDY DIED BUT HIS VISION WILL SURVIVE

I can't pass a homeless person or an abandoned building without thinking about my dad's passion regarding people without shelter. He was an intelligent man who not only had his heart wide open but his eyes as well. He wasn't oblivious to those who chose to do nothing with their lives and eventually ended up on the streets; but he realized that homelessness shouldn't be stereotyped because on any given day, any one of us could find ourselves in the same predicament.

The fact of the matter is that it rains on the "just" the same as it does on the "unjust." He realized that everyone who lives on the streets is not there because they are lazy and contribute nothing to the world. He understood they weren't just "uninspired litter" on the sidewalk or park bench in need of a shower. He saw them for who they are still today: somebody's child, somebody's parent, somebody's grandparents, somebody's sibling, somebody's relative, somebody's friend, someone who used to be an honor student, the president of the PTA, a nana or a papa, a favorite sister or brother, a very successful relative or friend. I always say that we shouldn't throw the baby out with the bath water.

I learned from my dad that people shouldn't be judged by their circumstances. If there is someone outside of a restaurant, no way should we, if able, go in and order food for ourselves without thinking about them.

Matthew 25:35-37 (NIV)

35 For I was hungry, and you gave me something to eat, I was thirsty and you gave me something to drink, I was a stranger and you invited me in, 36 I needed clothes and you clothed me, I was sick and you looked after me, I was in prison and you came to visit me 37 Then the righteous will ask Him, "Lord, when did we see you hungry and feed you, or thirsty and give you something to drink? 38 When did we see you as a stranger and invite you in, or needing clothes and clothed you? 39 When did we see you sick or in prison and go to visit you? 40 The king will reply 'Truly I tell you, whatever you did for one of the least of these brothers and sisters of mine, you did for Me.' (Biblical, Inc.)

Honestly, how could we miss the meaning of these verses of Scripture? It breaks my heart when traveling through cities and seeing churches on almost every corner while people are within eyeshot sleeping on sidewalks—men, women, girls, boys sleeping in the heat of day or cold of night. It seems like the fundraisers could sometimes be about the less fortunate.

I remember one year while at Oak Grove Baptist Church on Mother's Day, I was led to have a Mother's Day dinner there. The fellowship hall at the church was beautifully decorated and fit for the queens in attendance. I asked the members to adopt a mother from the nursing home and bring them to dinner. It was a beautiful affair. There were many tears shedded and faces of appreciation.

My maternal grandmother, Louisa, died of breast cancer when she was only forty-five. Watching my mother going into the room of her adopted mother and seeing her face light up at her adopted daughter brought tears to even my eyes. You can tell that the old lady took extra time with her appearance.

I am reminded of Luke 14:12-24 The Great Banquet—

In that scenario, Jesus said to His host, "When you give a luncheon or dinner, do not invite your friends, your brothers or sisters, your relatives, or your rich neighbors; if you do, they will invite you back and you will be repaid. But when you give a banquet, invite the poor, the crippled, the lame, the blind, and you will be blessed. Although they cannot repay you, you will be repaid at the resurrection of the righteous."

When one of those at the table with Him heard this, he said to Jesus, "Blessed is the one who will eat at the feast in the kingdom of God." Jesus replied: "A certain man was preparing a great banquet and invited many guests. At the time of the banquet, he sent his servant to tell those who had been invited, 'Come, for everything is now ready.'

"But they all alike began to make excuses. The first said, 'I have just bought a field, and I must go and see it. Please excuse me.' Another said, 'I have just bought five yokes of oxen, and I am on my way to try them out. Please excuse me.' Still another said, 'I just got married, so I can't come.'

"The servant came back and reported this to his master. Then the owner of the house became angry and ordered his servant, 'Go quickly into the streets and alleys of the town and bring in the poor, the crippled, the blind and the lame.'

"'Sir,' the servant said, 'what you ordered has been done, but there is still room.' Then the master told his servant, 'Go out to the roads and country lanes and compel them to come in, so that my house will be full.' I tell you, not one of those who were invited will get a taste of my banquet."

Jesus taught that when people gather, they should not just invite those who they know and who are like them. He told them to invite those who are poor, crippled, lame and blind. Jesus said that if they do this then they will be blessed. When they invite people to their gatherings who cannot return the favor, then they would be blessed in ways they were not expecting—ways they were not looking for.

Through this teaching, Jesus was restoring divisions between people and those who were marginalized. He went on to tell a parable where those who have worldly riches don't come to the dinner they're invited to. They're distracted by their worldly riches and responsibilities, so people with disabilities are invited instead.

Even though it is clearly stated and should be understood, it seems that God's Plan is often misconstrued. There's very little seeking God's Will and an overindulgence of seeking our own. We lean towards feeding pearls to the swine—the swine of greed rather than to the vessel of need. We pour into overflow rather than into emptiness. How do we miss the hunger, thirst, immobility, as well as loneliness and pursue pouring into fullness which inevitably becomes waste? Many people's greed has caused them to be spiritually constipated; their intestinal and detestable temples are filled to its capacity, and they're still yearning for more. Why can't those who are able to fill see the deficit; why are we mopping up messes that could be fillers for empty vessels?

My dad witnessed this. Seeing God's people forsaken vexed his entire being. He couldn't look upon need and walk away from it as if it didn't exist. He carried burdens that could have been lighter had they been shared.

This is why I believe God is positioning me to receive the mantle and complete the work Daddy began. I cannot only see one homeless shelter; I see various ones. I see churches renovating vacant buildings for the unsheltered. I see feeding ministries including the shelters on their grocery lists. I see businesses like Lowe's and Home Depot donating outdoor play equipment. I see grocery stores making weekly deliveries to shelters. I see buses picking up children to take them to get their shots and teeth cleanings. I see so many beautiful things in my mind's eyes, and it is my prayer that others will see it too.

My definition of a household of faith is a house where the occupants believe in the God that promises never to leave nor forsake them. Can you imagine the churches reversing some curses by tithing 10% of its earnings to do as the book of Matthew commands? Feeding the sheep not only the Word of God but the mighty actions of God as well. I would rather see a testimony than to hear one. The Bible is filled with Truth, but it is also filled with instructions.

It's the Christian's manual. Yes, social services exist, and it was put in place for the people in need because the poor will always be among us. However, if the benevolence of God's people, people who are called by His Name, would look beyond the church house and see the church's mission, our temporary home here on earth wouldn't feel like hell on earth. No, this is not our permanent home, but it is our home until God calls our name.

When I speak of benevolence, I am not only speaking financially; there are some gifts that can be shared to strengthen our brothers and sisters in order for them to pay it forward. If you are an electrical engineer, take someone who dreams about becoming an electrician under your wing; mentor and teach them so that they are now strengthened to help someone else.

There are people living in mansions who have no clue of what a homemade biscuit tastes like. Teach a willing individual the art of biscuit making to be a blessing to a family. Every gift that God gives is priceless and there is a place for it. There are cooks, seamstresses, nannies, gardeners, teachers, singers, writers, manual laborers, church school teachers, Bible scholars, architects, construction workers, salespeople, housekeepers, beauticians, makeup artists, designers, landscapers, builders and every possible career you can think of lying on the sidewalks of America. Suffolk could be the city to get the ball rolling. We have the opportunity and the power to give the catchphrase "Surprising Suffolk" new meaning. Somebody's got to lead so that others may follow.

My spirit is bursting with anticipation as I reflect on the Word as proclaimed in 1 Corinthians 2:9 (NIV), "But as it is written, Eye hath not seen, nor ear heard, neither have entered into the heart of man, the things which God hath prepared for them that love him." I truly believe in the promises of God. He is not a man who can lie. I have no idea of how God is going to use me, and I am absolutely clueless as to what His plan looks like, but there's an unexplainable peace that I can rest assured that it is already done. I'm excited and available!

Lawrence

Continued from page 1

for Suffolk's underprivileged.

"He was in such a jolly mood yesterday," said his daughter, Judy Chapman. "It's so untimely, but he accomplished so much in his life. He lived a rich, full life, and he worked until the day he died."

At 68, Lawrence had battled illness and injuries from another car accident in the last year. But his daughter, who lived with her father, said he was feeling good: he was active and looking forward to the upcoming City Council elections.

Lawrence's death leaves two challengers – William H. Goodman and Wong-ya G. Jones – to vie for the Cypress borough seat held by Vice Mayor Ronald O. Hart.

During his run for council, Lawrence cited improvements in education and upgraded housing as a major goal, and also stressed the importance of developing a shelter

to temporarily serve those without housing.

"The lack of a shelter for our homeless here in Suffolk borders on criminal negligence," Lawrence noted in January. "There are a number of old buildings here in the city which are not being used for a thing, and that makes no sense at all when there are people who need shelter."

When Lawrence announced his candidacy Jan. 4, he stressed his friendship with Hart and said, "I'm not running against anyone. I'm running for a position on City Council."

Hart said last night he and Lawrence had a close relationship, and called Lawrence "a very intelligent man who has been able to accomplish a lot. This community and this city should be so proud of him."

CHAPTER NINETEEN

IS THERE NO BALM IN GILEAD (SUFFOLK)?

That is the question for the city of Suffolk. Is there no balm there? I represent one of the souls that needed healing. I've heard it said that you can't be healed in the place where you've been hurt. I'm not ready to accept that as fact—without consideration of other factors, namely God. I tend to believe that the place of your pain can be the perfect location for your healing. That is a perfect opportunity for God to be glorified because it gives those who witnessed your hurt to now see how God turned it around for your good. It's a visual testimony and it gives hope!

By definition, balm is associated with healing, whether in the natural or used metaphorically. It could be for lips that are chapped, or it could be a bowl of your mother's homemade soup when you aren't feeling well.

In regards to a city, there may be areas in need of healing. When there is generation after generation of impoverished families, there is a need for healing. Metaphorically speaking, having one member of the family to make the decision to complete his or her education or learn a trade could be the balm to heal poverty in present and upcoming generations. When there is racism that has been generational, there is a need for healing. Creating spaces that appeal to the desires of all cultures in order to provide education and entertainment could be the balm to eradicate separatism. There is a need for healing when there has been no growth in certain areas such as homeless shelters. Churches and organizations partnering to provide a place to clear the parks and streets of human beings sleeping in the cold and heat could be the balm to create the environment that God alludes to when He says that "what we do for the least, we do unto Him."

Suffolk has moved from decades before to the present with many improvements along the way, but the work remains incomplete. There are so many missed opportunities. Many families are attracted to "Peanut City" and want to build a life there, but we could go far beyond just building new structural aspects of communities. It could become the city where each and every citizen, no matter the color, ethnicity, race, gender, religion, political affiliation or social status, would be assisted in living a rich and fulfilling life. To neglect seeking the capabilities of the people who live there may be a disservice to the city. There are too many unexplored treasures lying dormant on the streets, park benches, and in disabled cars. There are gifts that remain unopened because the package is not appealing. It behooves us to look deeper because we may be looking down or pass someone who could possibly benefit Suffolk's future.

There is 20/20 vision when it comes to the capable elite and proverbial cataracts pertaining to the willing downtrodden. We have to humble ourselves before God. He looks beyond the outer appearance and sees the heart. Many hearts through life have been shattered—hearts that once were CEOs in Corporate America, doctors, lawyers, educators, singers, preachers, great parents, humanitarians, stock brokers, phenomenal chefs, irreplaceable nannies and housekeepers—the list goes on and on. Many of us fear the possibility of ever being on the streets, but we must be careful because we often attract the very thing we fear.

On a personal note, there were four major things I've always feared: diabetes, cancer, losing a parent, and losing a child. I have experienced all four. So now, when thoughts arise that induce fear, I begin to thank God that it is not so. I used to say the words, "I couldn't imagine" and now I realize how easily my inability to imagine could become a reality.

People have often complimented me on my intelligence, and I appreciate the compliments, but intelligence can't compare to wisdom. Wisdom is something that can't be attained in a classroom or from a textbook. You can have a third-grade education and be one of the wisest people in the world! Life teaches you, and then it tests you.

There's something grand about being tried and tested; when deliverance takes place, there's a feeling of refinement—much like the purification process of gold or the pressures associated with a diamond. With that being said, how many of us would see a golden nugget or a diamond ring on the sidewalk and ignore it? Yet, isn't that what many of us are doing? *We* could be the balm to bring massive healing to a city that has so much great potential. As it is rich in land, it could be just as rich in humanitarianism.

Selah

CHAPTER TWENTY

MY MOTHER'S DOUBLE PORTION

Even in my youth, I have always said that I will make sure my parents were well taken care of because I understood that I was their only child. There were no siblings to meet together to come up with a strategic plan; I was it—I was the plan. However, seeing myself as their caregiver was somewhat incomprehensible to me at the time because they were the ones who provided me with everything I needed and desired. I was that child who when asked, "What would you like for Christmas?" was clueless as to how I would respond.

Had my dad not died, I would still be at 115 Carver Avenue, Suffolk, VA, 23434 with phone number 539-8135. I would still be timing dinner for when he came home from work. I would still be in the hallway talking to Mama on the phone while she's asking the sizes of the kids or ranting about one thing or the other. She was the feisty one but with a heart of gold.

I often think about how I would have attended to my parents. I would have let Daddy remain downstairs in his little apartment with our sound system to communicate; my mother in the bedroom coming up from the apartment, and my bedroom across the hall from her. Oh, what a beautiful vision! We would have our meals in the kitchen with Daddy and I drinking coffee and Mama drinking tea. Daddy would have his black with three sugars. I would have decaf with three Splendas and three creams, and Mama would have her tea with five sugars. The news would be on the kitchen television. My kids would be making breakfast as I get to enjoy starting my day off with my parents. I would have Adrian (RIP), Jamie or Allen to help Daddy with dressing. Nichole or I would help Mama.

The kids would then have breakfast, after which they would bring the kitchen back together. I would get the *Suffolk News Herald* from the mailbox, give it to Mama to read while Daddy watched the television downstairs; after which I would take the newspaper to him. They would either be brought to the front porch or rolled around Oakdale depending on what they wanted to do. I would be housecleaning, paying bills, making a grocery list and doing laundry. When things were done and they were settled, probably tired, they would nap while I wrote another book.

At noon, they would have lunch, and I would be the one preparing it. When my parents were back to their room of choice, I would crawl into my recliner to watch the *Young & The Restless* and the *Bold & Beautiful*. I would set it on record in case I dozed off.

After dinner, we would probably gather in the den or living room to talk and watch television together. Next, we would all prepare for bed and retire around 8 pm. I would go downstairs to tuck Daddy in with a kiss; come upstairs to do the same with Mama; say goodnight and kiss my children before retiring. I promise you that this vision constantly plays in my head, which is why I don't see caring for my mother as a burden; it is a privilege.

My heart goes out to those who have neither of the people who brought them into the world. The emotions that come over me are surreal to say the least, when I see my mother's tummy, realizing that I once lived there or when I help her with her hygiene, that it was once what she did for me.

My dad was my hero and the person I could tell anything to and not be judged. The one who passed on to me writing skills and the love of poetry. The one who helped me with homework and who taught me not to hate history because it will be a benefit to know the past in order to guide me in the present as well as the future. The one who taught me that he wasn't my God, and that it was God who brought us together as father and daughter.

It blew me away to know how much love and compassion a man of such small stature could carry in his heart, not just for me but for people—even for people who didn't love or have compassion for him. I can't help but wonder what his life would have looked like as he grew older and less accommodating. Would the phone or the doorbell still be ringing? Would he still be held in high regard or respected? God knew that the same people for which he advocated, whether it was financially, social-emotionally—or simply fighting for their civil rights, would erase him. Was his death a tragedy or a new trajectory? Would his family have been embraced or subsequently erased also?

As his daughter, I know the feeling of being erased, as I live and breathe. In the very same city, I know the feeling of being patted on the back and given accolades only to be rejected and scorned after I could no longer serve. As much as I miss Daddy, I thank God that he was spared the removal of covers and the exposure of the wolves in sheep's clothing. He didn't have to witness the people he loved only remembering his shortcomings and completely erasing the goodness that was mostly who he was. I realize in this season of my life that in order for some people to clear their conscience, they have to demonize others. They have to justify their own shortcomings by projecting their own negativity onto others.

Knowing my dad, he would have flicked it off of his shoulders and kept it moving. This is my inspiration and motivation to forget those things which are behind me and press (Phillippians 3:13-16)! Not only did he teach me servitude; he taught me fortitude. I've fallen along the way, but by God's mercy, I was able to get back up. I have some battle scars, but I wear them as badges of honor. As it was once said, "Throw me to the wolves and I'll return leading the pack." The weapons that were formed against me served as a foundation; they provided me with the footing I needed to boldly stand. Sometimes, what we blame on the devil is actually Spiritual Boot Camp. He gets no credit because I am fully aware that what he intended for evil, God means for my good.

These are the thoughts that empower me as I attend to the needs of my mother. She is receiving her portion as well as my dad's because he is where the wicked cease from troubling; and his weary soul is at rest. They're my parents and are the reason for my existence; I was conceived by them and created by God.

CHAPTER TWENTY-ONE

DADDY'S LAST DAY

After hours of the medical team at Obici Memorial Hospital trying to resuscitate my dad through heart massages—the heart that was so full of love and compassion, the heart that was headed to Lowe's to purchase building materials for a financially unable senior couple in Lake Kennedy whose roof was leaking—stopped beating. The expense of it was to come from his own pockets. He was going to hire builders to make the repairs. He was taking his lunch hour to do this beautiful benevolent act. He turned down my offer to make lunch for him when he stopped by our home en route. He was on a mission. My dad, who always gave of himself, was now gone. How could he be gone?

Memories of me standing at the window looking out at the man who was my world and thinking about how much I loved him. I was thinking about his unfiltered affection for me. I will never forget the last time I saw him. It was drizzling rain, he was wearing a cap, and I was wearing a Michael Jackson long-sleeved tee shirt.

After he pulled out of the driveway, I have memories of covering my head with my hands in an effort to protect myself from the rain and grabbing the newspaper out of the mailbox. I was standing in the living room and had begun reading the article about him as a candidate for the city council that I had written for the Suffolk News Herald.

My heart skips a beat when I remember the doorbell ringing, interrupting my reading and being told by our neighbor that Daddy had just been hit on Portsmouth Boulevard which was probably a three-minute drive from our home.

I had no memories of the minutes after hearing that. The next memory was approaching the accident, seeing my friend and classmate, Clarence, standing in the middle of the road and telling me not to approach the car that Daddy was in. He instructed me to go directly to the hospital and give them the information that they would need. He must have been very convincing because thinking back, to leave my dad there without going to him is incomprehensible.

I remember using the telephone booth to call someone; I don't remember who, but I will never forget hitting the booth so hard with my fist that it immediately began to swell. I remember seeing my choir director, Willie, and his wife, Terri. I have no memory of what they said to me. Sitting in that small room, waiting was like an out-of-body experience. Mrs. Diggs, a family friend and

Daddy's co-worker, kept us informed as the medical team worked tirelessly to revive him. I will never forget her coming to us and explaining the procedure; she then informed us that he didn't make it. Mrs. Diggs, years later, became the great grandmother of my first grandchild, Jasmine.

"God no! No way is the person I love most in the world, the strongest man I know, the one whose love I never doubted, the one who takes care of me and keeps me grounded, the biggest threat to anyone who dared to hurt or mistreat me, my educator, my buddy, my go-to person, my reason for choosing to live in Suffolk, my everything! No way are you telling me that he has been taken away from us!"

I have memories of leaving the hospital and pulling into my driveway with Rev. Sylvia pulling in right behind me. She grabbed hold of me and held me as my soul crashed. It was her birthday. I don't remember what she said to me either or when she left. My body, mind, and spirit literally shut down on me. My eyes saw, but my heart couldn't comprehend what was happening. I felt that the only way I would be able to endure the pain was to die myself. However, I immediately began to think about leaving my children in that kind of pain. That thought caused me even more pain.

That evening, our home was filled with people offering their condolences. Again, I remember some faces but not much more. I do remember one of our church members, Gladys Lawrence, coming in and seeing me wrapped in Daddy's jacket and saying "I knew she would be like this." There were two things that somewhat soothed the pain; they were my dad's scent from his jacket and the fact that three days before, he had rededicated his life to God.

On his last day, he stepped into eternity and received honor from the "Promise Keeper." Unlike the event that took place at Chorey Andrew Apartments which was designed to "honor" his memory. Our family sat together in front of the building and listened to people speaking about what a blessing he was to the city of Suffolk. A plaque was designed that was to be hung in the recreation room of the development. Ironically, my sister moved there years later, and there was no sign of the plaque. It had been removed or more accurately—erased.

Although people tried to erase my dad from the pages of history, he can never be erased from the hearts of those lives he touched. He was a change agent, who was instrumental in the progression of helping people enrich their lives, thus enriching the city of Suffolk. He didn't give up on people; he believed in them and their abilities to achieve even their wildest dreams. He was a giver, a motivator; he was supporting, kind, inspirational, sincere, committed, vigilant, a rebel of his time who stood up for the voiceless. Because of my dad, I stand tall today and teach my children and grandchildren the importance of using their voices and taking a stand for what they believe in. I believe in helping others, and this is a legacy that my dad left us, and I will never let his memory die.

CHAPTER TWENTY TWO

"I" WITNESS

(The childhood memories and account of his grandson, Allen Lawrence Boddie-Chapman)

March 19, 1986, started like any other rainy day in Suffolk, Virginia. I remember the sound of raindrops tapping on the roof of the school bus, almost like a gentle reminder to slow down and appreciate the quiet. But I was far too excited for that. I couldn't wait to get off the school bus and head to the open field across from our house. My grandfather, James Lawrence, had big plans for that space. He wanted to turn it from a dense, overgrown area into a playground for all the neighborhood kids. He believed every child deserves a safe place to run and play, away from the troubles that often surrounded us.

Grandfather was a man of few words. He didn't say much at home, but his actions spoke volumes. He was a political leader, but more than that, he was a loving grandfather who devoted himself to our family and the community. He had a knack for helping everyone he met. I often thought we had more than we needed because he made sure of it. There were countless times he'd stop by the bread store and load up on bags of cakes, pies, and other treats. I can still picture those giant contractor-sized trash bags overflowing with sweets. My job was to clear out the cabinets just to make room for it all.

It was more than just the snacks, though. It was his way of sharing joy and kindness with everyone around him. He couldn't stand wasting food. I can hear him now, saying, "There are children in third-world countries who would love to eat the food you are wasting." That phrase stuck with me, shaping how I viewed the world. He taught us to appreciate what we had and to be mindful of those less fortunate.

My mother was truly the apple of his eye. He loved her deeply, and you could see it in the way he treated her. But when it came to us kids, he had his own unique way of showing love.

I remember my sister Millie would always be excited when he caught her reading. For every book she finished, he'd hand her a crisp twenty-dollar bill. "Keep reading, Millie," he'd say, a smile creeping onto his face. He believed education was the key to a better life, and he wanted us to know that learning could be fun.

He was also generous to those in need. If he learned that a senior citizen needed help with their home, like a new roof, he wouldn't hesitate to dip into his own savings to help. He cared deeply for our community, and his actions reflected that.

But on that rainy day, everything changed. When I got home, I sensed something was off. My mother's face was pale, her eyes filled with tears. My heart sank as she told me my grandfather had passed away. I felt like the ground had disappeared beneath my feet. The man who had taught me so much, who had given me so many wonderful memories, was gone.

In the years since that day, I've often reflected on his legacy. James Lawrence was not just my grandfather; he was a hero to many. He promoted literacy and encouraged young people to strive for more. I see his spirit in my children now—their creativity, intelligence, and determination. They read with the same passion Millie did, and I hope to inspire them with the same love of learning that he instilled in us.

Looking at the news today, the crime and struggles in Suffolk are heartbreaking. I remember how frustrated my grandfather was about the lack of places for kids to play. He knew that without safe spaces, children might find trouble instead of opportunities. His dreams for our community were rooted in a desire to give children a chance to grow up in a safe, nurturing environment.

Though he's no longer with us, his spirit lives on in me. I strive to carry forward his lessons of kindness, generosity, and the importance of education. My experiences with him have shaped my character, guiding me to help others just as he did. I often think of myself as an I-witness to his legacy, and it motivates me to make a difference in my own way.

Every time I see my children and grandson explore, read, and engage with the world, I feel his presence reminding me that love and action can truly change lives.

Selah

A WORD FROM THE AUTHOR

The book was written for the purpose of educating others regarding the importance of protecting and celebrating our legacies and to also help us to understand and appreciate the contributions that were made by the generations before us. Quite often, who we are is in direct correlation to someone who was in our lineage—those who we never had the opportunity to experience personally.

My maternal grandmother died from breast cancer when I was three months old. My mother often laughs at me when I say things that her mother would have said. Things that would make one laugh. She saw her mother in me when I was actively working in the church or how I like things to be neat and clean. Just as I do now, she loved doing kind things for others and was attracted to those who were viewed as underdogs. She passed her love for fashion to my mother who passed that love to me. We share our love and passion for family. She also sought to bring everyone together. She was a survivor from many adverse situations, and was as resilient as I have found myself to be. So, even though I don't limit family relationships to DNA, there's no denying that it plays a huge part in our lives.

My son, Adrian, did not grow up with his biological dad, but as I watched him grow up, along with the facial resemblance came certain mannerisms of him. When his dad was eating and enjoying his food, he would gently tap the upper part of his ear; Adrian did it exactly the same way. That is probably something that only a mother would notice. Learned behavior does exist, but we cannot deny the power of DNA.

To that point, I see my father all the time: And my nephew, Travis, and my grandson, Julian's love for football; My youngest son, Allen and his passion for standing on what he believes; My grandson Justin's work with electricity; My granddaughter Allena's extreme intelligence and work ethics; My grandson Jordan's love for family; My beloved son Adrian's love for rhyme; My daughter Nichole's obsession with buying in bulk; My son Jamie's natural ability to attract people in his life and little things coming from so many of us, including my granddaughter Judea's creativity and relentless drive.

Last of all, me, who people have always said throughout my life, being the "spitting image" of him. Un-ERASED is only a chapter in the Lawrence Legacy. Chapters are being written every day at our visits, family gatherings, kids' sports games, childbirth experiences, sicknesses and yes, even death. That is why it means so much to me to be a presence in the lives of my family members. We cannot afford to take one second for granted. After God, comes family. As with the legacy that James Wesley Lawrence left behind, family is not defined by DNA, but by the divinely orchestrated relationship of those in the communities around us.

SPECIAL NOTE

Suffolk's Housing History—he was never mentioned as its first Housing Manager and Rehabilitation Inspector

1971-1974

City Council appointed Board of Commissioners George Y. Birdsong. George W. Scott, Rev. M.R. Boone, G. S. Hobbs and Marvin R. Stephenson designating George Birdsong as Chairman and Assistant City Manager C.M. Moyers as Temporary Secretary. The Commissioners met with the Planning Commission to discuss plans for public housing sites, the need for a zoning subdivision and minimum housing ordinances. An Organizational meeting was held on July 6, 1971 and the Bylaws and Seal were adopted. Mr. George Scott was elected Vice Chairman.

In 1974, the City of Suffolk merged with the City of Nansemond City Council and consolidated Nansemond Redevelopment and Housing Authority's and Suffolk Redevelopment and Housing Authority's Board of Commissioners. The new board consisted of George Y. Birdsong as Chairman. David Anderson C.M. Draper, Richard Harrell. G.S. Hobbs. W.E. Moody and Marvin R. Stephenson.

1976-1981

Cypress Manor/Parker Riddick Village. Named for Moses A. Riddick, Jr. (former member of the Nansemond County Board of Supervisors, former member of Suffolk City Council and former employee of SRHA) and Locke Parker (President of United Auto Workers [UAW] Local Union 26), Davis Boulevard, in the Cypress Manor Community, was named for Mr. Jasper Davis, an engineering consultant from Virginia Beach who suggested to Nansemond County officials to apply to the U.S. Department of HUD for participation in a rent subsidy program. Cogic Square, the street name of Cypress Manor Community, was named for the Church of God in Christ (COGIC) under the direction of Rev. D. Lawrence Williams. SRHA purchased Cypress Manor in 1976 and opened its doors in 1978. Parker village opened in 1981.

12 units of intermediary care for the mentally challenged know as the Finney Avenue Residence was constructed in 1979.

1984-1989

Hoffler Apartments which opened in 1984 was named for Dr. William M. Hoffler, Sr. who founded the first black hospital, Suffolk Community Hospital at the corner of Spruce Street and Madison Avenue, in 1942. Dr. Hoffler donated his home to First Baptist Church, Mahan Street, to be used as a convalescent home (First Baptist Hoffler Home for Adults) for ambulatory patients.

Colander Bishop Meadows which opened in 1986 was named for Bishop Obadiah Colander and Mr. King S. Bishop who organized neighborhood support groups in support of the public housing project in the Saratoga neighborhood.

Chorey Park Apartments which opened in 1987 was named for the Chorey Estates from which the land was purchased. Chorey Park houses the elderly, disabled and handicapped citizens of the City of Suffolk.

Five single-family homes were constructed in Saratoga through a partnership with Suffolk Habitat for Humanities in 1988.

ACKNOWLEDGEMENTS

There are several people, situations, and oppositional assignments that I must address that served as my motivation to write Un-ERASED: The Attempted Annihilation of the James Wesley Lawrence Legacy.

Before any other acknowledgments are noted, the first goes to my Source, my Strength, my Provider, my Sustainer, my Voice, my Peace, my Everything—my God. Had He not interrupted my sleep and arrested my thoughts, I never would have decided to write a nonfiction book filled with unadulterated truth. I continue to be God's secretary. He dictates while I take notes and record.

Next, I acknowledge my father (RIP) who was my best friend, my hero and cheerleader; my mother, who is also my cheerleader and who thinks of me as her gift to mankind (she always tells me that I gained my intelligence from my father); my youngest son, Allen, who motivates me to speak out and to take a stand unapologetically as well as being my ride or die; my daughter, Nichole, who constantly tells me how proud she is of me as I strive to guide her away from the very things that were designed to kill me and who spends countless hours researching on behalf of her grandfather; my oldest living son, Jamie, who makes me laugh when I feel like crying as well as being instrumental in providing me with the large family I've always wanted; and last but not least, my Adrian (RIP), my body's first surviving tenant…the first one to call me "Mama" as well as the one who made me a grandma to my beautiful grandchildren and great grandchildren, to which I'm either Gammy (Adrian), GiGi (Jamie), MiMi (Allen) or Nana (Nichole). I proudly wear each title. I love how you guys love me…each in your own special way. To my sister, Alisa (RIP), my only sibling, who looked up to me and made me want to be a better person as well as sharing the same wonderful dad.

To Pastor John Troy Blackwell for his endless encouragement, love and support.

To my neighbor who is an estate attorney, Sabrina Winters, for putting her Independence Day celebration on hold to come over, sit with me on my porch to give me clarity, support and guide me as I begin to tread unknown territory.

To Patricia Tyus, CEO at the Suffolk Redevelopment & Housing Authority…thank you for listening and hearing the stories of one of the pioneers who came before you. You didn't have a chance to meet my dad, but I pray that you will experience the fulfillment of his hopes and dreams for the housing authority. Thank you for consenting to a wall to be dedicated in his memory and to his honor. Your integrity is in line with your position there.

To Suffolk City Council who allowed me to be heard while I pled consideration for my father's legacy that had been erased. Many of you did not know my father but I believe you heard from my heart. A special thank you to Councilman Tim Johnson for his encouraging words and to Vice-Mayor Leroy Bennett who knew my father very well, speaking highly of him and encouraging his constituents to seriously consider my request.

To Monica, the receptionist Allen and I had the pleasure of meeting on one of our visits there. You are the first face seen upon entering, and you represent the SRHA well.

To Micheal Littlejohn, NC Civil Rights Attorney, who was unable to represent me as my attorney because he doesn't practice law in Virginia but placed me on the trajectory to resolutions.

To the situations of financial struggles, two fights with cancer, one being stage four and metastatic, three strokes, one in my inner ear and two on my brain, the losses, the persecutions, the rejections, the various levels of abuse, the disappointments, the exploitations, the insincere hugs and handshakes all played a part in giving me the determination I needed to lay aside every debilitating weight that bound and crippled me.

Had you not challenged me, I would have died a slow death of complacency. You showed me and others my strength, perseverance and ability to get back up, rise from the grave of despair, dust myself off and plant my feet firmly on the trajectory that leads me to my divine and ordained destiny. It took thirty-eight years of preparation.

How do I begin to share the extent of my appreciation to my publisher, Tara Tucker? To have the ability and opportunity to share my story is beyond a blessing, but to have a knowledgeable, professional, discerning, articulate publisher who has integrity and is authentic…work side by side with you is an experience I didn't see coming. I have been the author of several books and a participant in a few anthologies, and through my publishing experiences, I have been given a point of reference. I know the challenges of communication; it isn't always easy to share your heart literarily. Tara has been given the gift of compassion in addition to her other attributes. UnERASED wasn't a whim; it was an assignment…an assignment that required me to put aside any debilitating emotions. Her natural ability to draw from deep within her clients' hearts and to help put into words their innermost feelings is not only a skill; it's an anointed skill. If anyone is willing to step out on faith to tell their story, I recommend Tara, hands down.

To those who stood staunchly in opposition of giving honor where honor is due, you were my inspiration. Through you, I learned to push back and to push back hard! You were my proverbial footstool. You set me up for a comeback. Your covers were snatched away. I was given spiritual X-ray vision. When I looked to you for help, I saw through you. You smiled way too hard…so hard that your fangs were revealed. Your laughter was forced and was like chalk going across a blackboard. Your eyes, the windows to your soul, couldn't hide your disdain and desperation for my demise. As bad as it all sounds, you lifted me to remarkable heights and delivered me from incomprehensible depths. The fire that you sent my way purified my soul. Your gossiping conversations highlighted me so that the true Judy would be revealed. Thank you for that. I had lost myself and you reminded me of who and Whose I was. I couldn't have written this book without you.

Here's a Sneak Peek at my Next Book
"He Said That He Loved Me To Death: And He Did."

An abused woman's nightmare
Based on several true stories

HE TOLD ME HE LOVED ME TO DEATH: AND HE DID!
JUDY E. LAWRENCE LAMB

"Love should never leave you bruised, broken, or buried in silence."

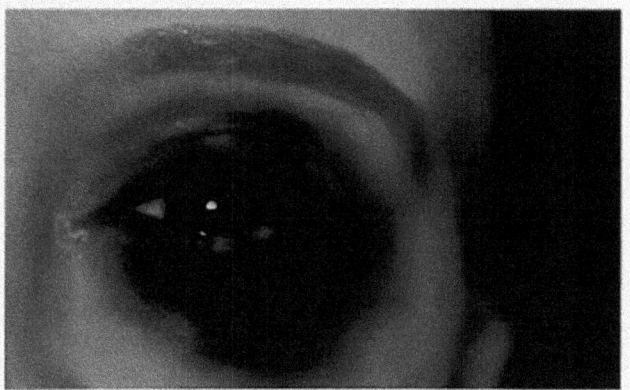

She thought his words meant forever.
She never imagined they meant her life.

This raw and riveting memoir reveals the hidden pain behind closed doors. Judy E. Lawrence Lamb courageously exposes the unspoken realities of domestic violence - the manipulation, the isolation, the wounds that run deeper than skin, and the love that killed.

- **Trigger Warning:** This story addresses graphic experiences of abuse and survival.

 Domestic Violence Awareness
No one deserves to be silenced by fear. If you or someone you know is experiencing abuse, reach out. There is help. There is hope.

Learn more at judywrites.com

PREFACE

It had been an exhausting weekend, and I was sleeping soundly. I'm not sure if I was dreaming or if I really heard a man angrily shouting and a woman screaming but I became fully awake. I texted myself notes and the beginning of a song for this book. The names have been changed to protect the possible deliverance of the guilty.

Song: You are my love. You are the love of my life. You've taken me beyond the limits of what love is supposed to be.

Statistics:

The NCADV is a grassroots, tax-exempt membership organization which works to stop violence against women and children. Established in 1978, NCADV is the only national organization of shelters and support services for battered women and their children.

CHAPTER ONE

"Hurry up, Naomi! We've got 4 hours on the road and orientation begins at nine! It's 4:30 and no telling what we may run into!"

My mother was an on time kind of person. She says if you get some place right on time, you're late.

Today is my first day at Bradley Mills University! We have been shopping and packing all summer. Grandma has made tins of cookies for my roommate and me to share. My roommate and I had gotten to know one another through FaceTime. Her name was Gretchen. We laughed because Grandma made enough cookies to feed everyone in the cafeteria for a month!

While Mama and I shopped until we dropped, Daddy was online shopping for my dorm room. Gretchen and I decided to use a collection of both of our favorite colors. Mine being hot pink and teal with hers being purple and yellow, it was to be a vibrant room for sure. We decided to use one of each of our favorites for the bathroom so it was to be teal and yellow.

Daddy had found the most adorable mini fridge, microwave and keurig set. They were to be delivered to our school on moving day along with other things I needed to make it home for the next four years. That was a great move to have them delivered since my shoes and clothes would take a lion's share of our SUV.

While Mama and I were bringing stuff downstairs, Grandma was making breakfast biscuits and pouring juice into thermos bottles. There was no time to stop and eat but we knew that it wouldn't be wise to attend orientation hungry. Growling stomachs can be annoying; especially if it's your stomach. Daddy was putting the suitcases and school supplies in the car.

At 5:50 AM, we were all settled in and ready to go when I remembered my favorite thing in all the world—my guitar! I jumped out of the car, went back to the house, ran up the stairs to my room and grabbed my baby from the window seat. Now I was ready to begin my new chapter.

The ride was pretty uneventful. After we ate, we all went into our individual head space. I whipped out my cell, Mama began flipping through her magazine, Daddy switched to his favorite radio station and Grandma, yes Grandma, thought four hours of knitting would just about complete one of the blankets she was working on for the homeless shelter. No way was her only grandchild going off to college, leaving her at home.

After a couple of hours, Daddy pulled into a service station to top off the gas tank and grab an energy drink. He asked if anyone needed to get out but of course, his mom, wife and daughter had no intention of using the restroom so he pulled over to a nice restaurant. He understood that if it wasn't an emergency, we wouldn't feel as comfortable as he did using the service station restroom.

After everyone was back in the car, we got back on the road with two hours to go.

This time, within 20 minutes, everyone except Daddy was asleep so for the next two hours, the only sounds were R&B and gentle snores. At 8:50 AM, Daddy woke us up and announced that we were 10 minutes away from the school's auditorium. His three divas quickly sat up and began smoothing down their hair and popping mints.

Soon after, we saw a beautiful campus with green grass and trees, impressive buildings, and a big blue sign that said Bradley Mills University. Excitement filled the car as everyone started talking at once. We were given a pass to enter by a security guard who directed us to the dormitory. He welcomed our family and wished us well.

CHAPTER TWO

The parking lot was packed but things went along smoothly because the welcoming team was very efficient. We were shown the building where my dorm room was located. We decided to check out the room before we began unloading which wouldn't be a difficult task because they had a team of volunteers with carts to help us. We had to go through a pretty gate that opened up to a wide sidewalk leading us to my building which was named the Tubman Building. The door was propped open because it would automatically lock if closed. That was for added security for the students. Each dorm room also had a lock to which only the assigned student had access.

It was a beautiful fall day and excited chatter was all around us. After checking out the room, we returned to the car to begin unloading. It was a quick process but we all knew that the real work would begin once we got back to the room. My mother was very particular about everything having a place so throwing bags in the closet was not an option.We had bought shoe trees and hangers for my closet. Daddy had ordered shelving and cubicles for my personal items to avoid clutter in what turned out to be a small room. It was scheduled to be delivered between 10:00 AM and noon. The orientation in the auditorium was set to begin at 10:30 AM giving us the opportunity to at least empty our cars. Daddy had already been assured that if we are at orientation when the deliverers arrived, my belongings would be tagged and set outside the door.

Just as we were returning to our building, I heard someone call Gretchen's name. Thanks to FaceTime, I knew immediately that it was my roommate! We giggled, hugging and began jumping around in circles like two little girls who just met on the playground. With my things unloaded, we began helping Gretchen and her family.

I asked her which bed she would prefer and we agreed that it didn't matter because we'll be together no matter which bed we chose. I ended up choosing the bed by the window. Gretchen's bed was by the door. I was wondering why Grandma was carrying her knitting in such a large basket! It carried two embroidered blankets in the school colors for Gretchen and me! While Daddy was placing the furniture to accommodate our kitchen stuff, Mama was freshening up the bathroom and hanging our teal shower curtain. Grandma was tuckered out and sitting at my desk with her hands cupped under her chin watching the goings on.

It was 10:15 AM and time to walk over to the auditorium which was located nearby. We left everything as is, locked the door and the two families walked over together. Our parents shared what they did while we walked. My daddy shared that he was an optometrist. My mother shared that she was a dental assistant. Gretchen's parents owned a restaurant in New Hampshire. Grandma said she was a retired school teacher and is presently serving as support for our family. Once they arrived at the auditorium, they took their places in the long line. Grandma was grateful when she was offered a seat. It was placed by the entrance door so that she could join the others when we got to the front of the line. Finally, we were next in line. Grandma stood up, grabbed ahold of Naomi's arm and entered the building. There was a large open space with potted plants and showcases all around before going through the doors that led to the crowded room filled with intelligible conversations.

Daddy and Gretchen's dad led the way down to the front and found enough seats together for us. It was now 10 minutes to 11:00 AM, and people were coming onstage, adjusting microphones and checking the sound system. There were seats up there to be occupied by the presenters who would take turns coming to the podium and expounding on their individual areas of expertise.

It wasn't long before we heard the words "May I have your attention please?" There was an immediate silence and all occupants were looking towards the stage. It was the voice of the dean of students, Mr. Alexander.

The chairs were now occupied.

"We welcome you to Bradley Mills University and I speak on behalf of our entire staff when I say that we are honored that you chose this institution to prepare your child to enter a world of new beginnings. It is our pleasure to be given the opportunity to explore the potential of each and every student. We want to give you a bird's eye view of what the next four years of your children's academic trajectory will look like. However, our commitment to Bradley Mill's students is not limited to academics; we will also be actively involved in their growing pains, in them making wise choices, in teaching work ethics and time management as well as assisting them in seeing the value of a good and solid education. There will also be social events that will contribute to their socialization skills. We realize that our students have three areas that must be taken into consideration—not only their minds but their bodies and spirits as well. While this may be new to some; it will be reinforcement to others. With that being said, without further delay, I introduce to you, the head of security, Mr. George Weismann."

Mr. Weismann came to the podium, cleared his throat and began to speak.

"Good morning students and family of our freshman class. I, too, am honored to stand before you as I share the plan of security that has been orchestrated to ensure the safety and well being of our students here. We realize that one of your top priorities is that not only will your child receive a state of the art academic experience but their safety will also be our focus. There are several strategies in operation which includes a student hotline. Each student will be connected to the security team. There will always be double security when entering the dorms. All walkways are well lit with security cameras all around the campus. There will be no visitors on the grounds without clearance. SOS alarms will be in various places that will have a different sound than that of a fire alarm. Metal detectors are generously located throughout Bradley Mills both inside and outside of the buildings. We have underground protection in the event of a hurricane or other storms of destruction. My job is to keep our students safe. That is my one and only responsibility. My team consists of members who are just as committed to their safety. Are there any questions?"

Silence

"If all minds are clear, I will now introduce Mrs. Amy Forrester, a nutritionist, head of our cafeteria and the Vice President of Food and Nutrition Administration in our county." Beckoning her to come forward, he calls, "Mrs. Forrester?"

"I believe it is now noon, so good afternoon ladies and gentlemen. It is my responsibility to provide daily balanced meals three times a day for our students. I also prepare healthy snacks that are accessible throughout the day that may be something as simple as fruit or a salad. Due to my nutritional background, it is seldom that we have fast food even though it may be available in our cafeteria vending machines. I take into consideration that we have students who are vegan, vegetarian or have special dietary requirements. There will never be a day when a student has to be hungry because we are unable to accommodate their dietary needs. I suggest that while your child is here, they select a suitable meal plan to ensure that the inventory can accommodate the need. We only provide juices—both sugar-free and regular; however, sodas may be purchased also through the vending machines. Candy and other sweet treats will be sold at the student union. Does anyone have any questions for me?"

Silence

"Then I will introduce you to Dr. Carolyn Hector Thomas, who is the head of our nursing and emergency department. Dr. Thomas is an alumni of Howard University. She has been with us serving in this capacity for 12 years. Dr. Thomas?"

"Good afternoon folks. I'm pleased to meet you and I look forward to partnering with you as we seek to provide your student with the very best healthcare. I work very closely with Mrs. Forrester because I am a firm believer that dietary proactivity is the key to less health issues. My staff consists of highly qualified RNs, a nurses' assistant and a PA. The clinic is open 24-7 and is equipped for medical emergencies including 10 hospital beds. We have four janitors whose only responsibilities are to maintain the cleanliness and sanitation of the clinic. They perform round the clock sanitizing. We have our own pharmacists and pharmacy. They are responsible for the proper intake of any medication as well as the administration of topical medications."

After three hours of different departments being represented, the attendees were escorted to the cafeteria. There, they were served a delicious meal; after which, the students returned to the auditorium and the parents were released to return to their homes.

CHAPTER THREE

As Naomi re-entered the auditorium, she suddenly had butterflies in her stomach. She was anticipatory and excited—all at once. She took a seat on the front row because she didn't want to miss one word. The purpose of them being there was for roommates to be united at which time they would sit together for a lecture on respectfully coexisting. It was pretty basic stuff and the floor was opened for questions. It was cool because she and Gretchen already felt connected. After the meeting, the room was filled with excited chatter as the students, two by two made their exit.

Once outside, the girls began looking left to right deciding which direction led to their dormitory. Gretchen spotted a chapel which was the landmark she chose. The girls took off headed towards the chapel. Within five minutes, they were standing at the dorm. Gretchen took out her key and there they stood together bursting with pride as their eyes swept across the room. Naomi turned to Gretchen, she bowed and said, "Welcome to our new home for the next four years." Gretchen returned the bow with a "Thank you very much!"

After their ceremonial entrance, they went to work: packing, hanging, and folding. Their mutual taste for music made work feel like playtime. They were trying to get as much completed as they could before the 6:00 PM dinner bell.

They were practically done by 5:45 PM so they decided to head to the cafeteria before the bell rung. Gretchen suggested that they beat the crowd and avoid the long lines. It turned out to be a great suggestion because by 5:55 PM, there was a crowd standing at the cafeteria door. The girls looked out at the mass of students and gave each other a high five.

Dinner was pretty good and as the cafeteria manager told them at orientation, there was something there for everyone.

After dinner, the girls decided to walk around the campus for a while. There was so much to see so they decided not to wander too far from their dorm. They wanted to be back before dark. The plan was to finish up when we returned but after the wonderful meal and walk, all they wanted to do was shower and turn in. After their 'good nights,' the lights were off and the room was quiet by 8:30 PM.

For release date information and more, stay in touch with me via my website at JudyWrites.com.

ABOUT THE AUTHOR

Judy Eve Lawrence-Lamb is a native of New York and a long-time resident of a small town in Virginia (Suffolk). She now spends time with her mother Lucretia Lawrence, loving husband William, daughter, son-in-love, and granddaughter in Charlotte, North Carolina.

She was educated in both the New York public school system and Suffolk's public school system. After graduating from John F. Kennedy High School in Suffolk, she decided to attend Bronx Community College in New York before transferring to a university. However, many obstacles prevented her from completing those plans.

Judy married at 19 and had her first child at 21. As her children were born, dreams of completing her education became less of a priority. She is not only a stage four, metastatic breast cancer survivor who found herself in the fight again, Judy has survived three strokes, single-parenthood, rape, the sudden death of her first-born, Adrian, and her father, James in separate car accidents, domestic violence and many other events that would have caused a less determined individual to give up.

Judy has experienced many professions throughout the years, beginning at thirteen. She was a junior counselor at the Harlem Youth Division of the YWCA. As a student of Distributive Education in high school, she worked at Macy's in the shoe department. She was named DE Student of the Year in 1969. Once graduated, she went into banking and her first position was a teller at the former First National City Bank, now Citibank on Wall Street. Most of her jobs were centered around banking and retail.

Later she became employed at B. C. Harris Publishing Company where she worked for several years and quickly moved up within the company to trainer and manager. When she left, she returned to Macy's where she was named top performer in the district.

Finally, she began working in a field that she was very passionate about—education. She has served as both a teacher's assistant and a substitute teacher, which fulfilled another passion of hers—working with the youth.

She has authored several books and co-authored three anthologies. Judy has also authored poetry publications, lyrics, speeches, and stage plays. She worked for the newspaper in her city—Suffolk—the Suffolk News-Herald as a correspondent writer. Judy inherited her love for literacy from her father and she passed that love on to two of her children. Adrian was gifted in creating as well as performing rap and Allen followed his mother's footsteps in her diverse style of writing.

Finally, in 2009 she decided to return to college. She enrolled at Norfolk State University majoring in English. As she sat in the student union building one day after class waiting for her husband, her cell phone rang. It was her doctor informing her that she had breast cancer later finding out that it was stage four and metastatic.

She had to leave school for a while as she was unable to perform academically. The chemotherapy treatments were very aggressive. Once she completed chemotherapy, she had radiation to contend with. Even though she was extremely tired most of the time, she continued her studies at Norfolk State University, while simultaneously committing herself to an independent study at Norfolk Theological Seminary & College.

She knew at 45 that God was going to license her and send her out as an evangelist when she turned 60. Even though many tried to convince her to answer the call years before the time He gave her, she refused to move ahead of God. She preached her initial sermon December 18, 2011…13 days before her 60th birthday.

Judy graduated Magna Cum Laude from Norfolk State University in May 2013 with a BS degree alongside her youngest son who was a single father of three daughters and an adopted son who was also his nephew. She graduated summa cum laude from Norfolk Theological Seminary and College in June 2014, pursuing a Masters in Divinity.

She is CEO of Wesleys & Eves Corporation—Un-ERASED, special needs caregiver and developmental editor at Tucker Publishing House, LLC. She is also a literacy character, Grandma Judy Eve, who engages in literary programs for children.

She is the mother of four biological children: the late Adrian W. Boddie, James B. Boddie, Allen L. Boddie-Chapman and Nichole L. Boddie-Hopson, (as of the publishing of this book, 32 grandchildren and 16 great-grandchildren), Curtis III, Adriana, Nylah, Karson, Jase, Daylen, Kennedy, Journee, Morgan, Destinee, Wesley, Malachi, Kyzeir, Londyon, Kei'lani, Zariah and Adrian.

Her family was blessed with 5 children through her union with her husband, William—William Jr., Michelle, Nadine, Darrell, and Brian. Grandchildren—Chase, Antoine, Breya, Keristan, Derrick, Darell, LaShonda, Alisha, Malik and Corey (RIP).

Email: healedone59@yahoo.com
Website: judywrites.com
YouTube : Grandma Judy Eve Productions
@grandmajudyEve

www.ingramcontent.com/pod-product-compliance
Lightning Source LLC
Chambersburg PA
CBHW051622120626
46551CB00014B/1912